AP

Ca

to today's Questions

CREED	SACRA-MENTS
MORALS	PRAYER

Fr. Marcus Holden MA (Oxon), STL

Fr. Andrew Pinsent MA (Oxon), DPhil, STB, PhL, PhD

Catholic Truth Society

The main reference sources for this booklet are the Bible and the *Catechism of the Catholic Church*. All Scriptural citations are taken from the Revised Standard Version (RSV) Catholic Edition unless the following abbreviations are shown: NRSV, for a citation from the New Revised Standard Version; NJB for a citation from the New Jerusalem Bible. The abbreviation "ccc." followed by a number indicates a particular paragraph from the *Catechism*.

The publisher acknowledges permission to reproduce the following:- Pg 8: Albert Einstein with Robert Millikan and Georges LeMaitre © Bettmann/CORBIS. Pg 10: Gregor Mendel © Bettmann/CORBIS. Pg 14: Inscribed Tablet © David Rubinger/CORBIS. Pg 18: Rylands Papyrus Reproduced by courtesy of the University Librarian and Director, The John Rylands University Library, The University of Manchester. Pg 22: The Pilate Stone © istockphotos. Pg 26: Negative of the Turin Shroud © Sygma/Corbis. Pg 30: The Holy Trinity with St. John the Baptist, Mary Magdalene, Tobias and the Angel, c.1490-95 (tempera on panel), Botticelli, Sandro (1444/5-1510)/© Samuel Courtauld Trust, Courtauld Institute of Art Gallery,/The Bridgeman Art Library. Pg 34: View of Bernini's canopy and the dome of St. Peter's Basilica from the basement © Kazuyoshi Nomachi/Corbis. Pg 38 John Henry Cardinal Newman. Pg 42: Our Lady of Guadalupe, patroness of the Americas and protector of the unborn. Pg 46: The Last Supper or, The Communion of the Apostles, 1474 (oil on panel), Joos van Gent (Joos van Wassenhove) (fl.1460-75)/Galleria Nazionale delle Marche, Urbino, Italy, Alinari/The Bridgeman Art Library. Pg 50: The Baptistry of Paros Cathedral, Greece © Roger Wood/CORBIS. Pg 54: Eucharistic miracle in Siena © Santuario delle Sacre Particole. Pg 58: Pope Benedict XVI in the confessional 2007 © Pool/L'Osservatore Romano/Corbis. Pg 62: Blessed Louis and Zelie Martin. Pg 66: The Temptation of Christ by Duccio di Buoninsegna © the Frick Collection NY USA. Pg 70: C. S. Lewis © Getty Images. Pg 74: Mother Teresa in 2002 © Reuters/Corbis. Pg 78: Tabletop of the Seven Deadly Sins and the Four Last Things (oil on panel), Bosch, Hieronymus (c.1450-1516)/Prado, Madrid, Spain, Giraudon/The Bridgeman Art Library. Pg 82: Pope John Paul II on Tour in York, England 1982 © Louie Psihoyos/Science Faction/Corbis. Pg 86: The Mocking of Christ with the Virgin and St. Dominic, 1442 (fresco), Angelico, Fra (Guido di Pietro) (c.1387-1455)/Church of San Marco, Florence, Italy,/The Bridgeman Art Library. Pg 90: Agony in the Garden, Bellini, Giovanni (c.1430-1516)/National Gallery, London, UK,/The Bridgeman Art Library. Pg 98: Return of the Prodigal Son, c.1668-69 (oil on canvas), Rembrandt Harmensz. van Rijn (1606-69)/Hermitage, St. Petersburg, Russia,/The Bridgeman Art Library. Pg 102: The Virgin in Prayer, 1640-50 (oil on canvas) by Il Sassoferrato (Giovanni Battista Salvi) (1609-85) National Gallery, London, UK/Bridgeman. (For those images where the publisher has been unable to identify the copyright holder, any information would be gratefully received).

Contents

Creed

Sacraments

3

Morals

Prayer

A Prayer of St Thomas Aquinas
who always prayed before study

Bestow upon me, O God, an understanding that knows you, wisdom in finding you, a way of life that is pleasing to you, perseverance that faithfully waits for you, and confidence that I shall embrace you at the last. Amen.

Introduction

St Peter tells us, "*Always be prepared to make a defence to any one who calls you to account for the hope that is in you, yet do it with gentleness and reverence*" (1 Pet 3:15). Today, as in the time of the early Christians, people are intrigued by the Catholic Faith and often have many difficult questions to ask. Just as the first readers of St Peter's letter were called to respond, we are also called to explain and defend the faith in our own age.

To assist with this mission, this pocket guide presents a series of difficult questions and possible ways in which these questions might be answered from a Catholic perspective. The guide draws its material from Scripture, Tradition and Church teaching, especially the *Catechism of the Catholic Church*. Like the *Catechism*, this guide is also structured in a fourfold way: Creed, Sacraments, Morals and Prayer. The twenty-five individual sections, containing eighty-eight questions, follow the same structure as the *Evangelium* course and *Credo* pocket catechism, also published by the Catholic Truth Society.

This guide will be helpful to anyone who has questions about the Catholic Faith, especially those involved in evangelisation, missionary work and teaching. In addition, this booklet may help members of the Church who wish to deepen or refresh their own knowledge of the faith. Finally, the questions and answers of the booklet may be a great help in assisting both teachers and participants in catechetical courses, such as those connected with the *Rite of Christian Initiation for Adults* (RCIA).

Fr Georges Lemaître, 'Father of the Big Bang', with Albert Einstein
12 January 1933

This Catholic priest, Fr Georges Lemaître, proposed what is now known as the 'Big Bang' theory of the origin of the Universe. He also proposed ways in which astronomers might test this theory. Lemaître's life and work help refute the popular belief in a conflict between science and the Catholic faith.

The Meaning of Life

CREED

The meaning of life refers to the most fundamental reasons for the existence of the world and ourselves.

Can I ask difficult questions on issues regarding the Catholic faith?

Yes, it is good for both students and teachers to ask all kinds of questions about the Catholic faith, as Jesus shows us in the Gospels, "*After three days they found him [Jesus] in the temple, sitting among the teachers, listening to them and asking them questions; and all who heard him were amazed at his understanding and his answers*" (Lk 2:46-47). Questioning is important because, as Jesus tells us, "*The kingdom of heaven is like treasure hidden in a field*" (Mt 13:44). In other words, we have to work to uncover the mysteries of the kingdom of heaven, a task which in practice involves questioning and thinking through the implications of what God has revealed to us in our faith.

Why do many people believe that God does not exist?

There can be many reasons why *some* people do not believe that God exists. Nevertheless, *most* people do, in fact, believe in God, understood as some kind of 'first cause' of all other things. Indeed, the very fact that the word 'God' has some meaning in every major human language is indirect evidence that belief in God is natural for human beings. What is more, the existence of God is not, as is sometimes implied, a belief held exclusively by childish or uneducated persons. Among the great philosophers, scientists, writers and artists whose works affirm some kind of belief in God, one can include Plato, Aristotle, Augustine, Aquinas, Dante, Descartes, Michelangelo, Leonardo da Vinci, Kant, Newton, Cauchy, Newman, Einstein and Mendel. This list includes some of the most subtle and creative thinkers in human history, including pioneers of entire disciplines of science and some of the greatest artists. In addition, many philosophers, both ancient and modern, have offered arguments for the existence of God.

Furthermore, many people who claim to be atheists, rejecting belief in God, do, in fact, believe in an alternative 'first cause'. Either they claim that the universe is its own cause or that the universe is generated by some automatic or random process from a larger, invisible reality, such as a *multiverse*. In other words, many atheists propose an impersonal *substitute* for God rather than simply rejecting the existence of God outright.

Finally, a person's stance regarding the existence of God may have a moral aspect. It is true, of course, that many people who believe in God still to do evil, and some people commit terrible evil in the name of God. Nevertheless, to deny God's existence entirely changes the framework of morality. If there is no divine lawmaker to fear or heavenly Father to love, there is also no higher judge than oneself or the state for how one should treat one's fellow human beings. As a practical consequence, as Dostoevsky and others have pointed out, *everything is permitted*. While such a world might seem attractive to some, those states governed by atheist ideologies in the twentieth century, which killed some one hundred million people, show the risks consequent upon such thinking.

Hasn't modern science shown that human beings are simply clever animals?

Modern science has not shown that human beings are simply clever animals, if, by 'clever', we mean that all the intellectual abilities of human beings are found in other animals in less developed forms. Indeed, the very existence of science stands as a witness to the uniqueness of human beings, since other animals lack science at all. One could point to an almost infinite variety of other human activities, such as painting the Sistine Chapel or flying to the moon, to highlight the extraordinary uniqueness of human beings. The philosopher Wittgenstein expressed the difference as follows: a dog knows its master, but a dog cannot know that its master is coming home the day after tomorrow. In other words, other animals lack the ability to think of concepts like 'the day after tomorrow' or any abstract ideas, such as justice, truth and love. So non-human animals have no art, ethics, science, philosophy or anything involving such conceptual abilities.

Furthermore, as G. K. Chesterton pointed out (*Everlasting Man*, I.1), a bird can display great ingenuity in building a nest, but once the nest is built the bird is satisfied. The bird does not go on to develop architecture, art or to discuss the meaning of life. All non-human animals are satisfied to be what they are. The human person, by contrast, seeks ultimate happiness and is discontent with any finite, created things alone.

Further reading. *Compendium* questions 1-5; *Catechism* ccc. 27-43 covering: (i) the desire for God (ccc. 27-30); (ii) ways of coming to know God (ccc. 31-35); (iii) the knowledge of God according to the Church (ccc. 36-38); (iv) speaking about God (ccc. 39-43).

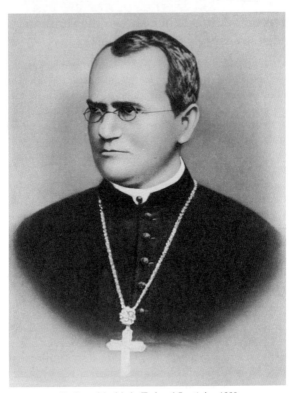

Fr Gregor Mendel, the 'Father of Genetics', c. 1880

Mendel's meticulous observations of the inherited characteristics of plants laid the foundations of modern genetics. Mendel also pioneered the systematic application of mathematics and statistics to biology, and his laws of inheritance revolutionised the cultivation of plants and the breeding of domestic animals. Mendel's work shows a Catholic appreciation of God's interaction with his Creation, articulated by St Thomas Aquinas, *"God has imparted to his creatures the dignity of being causes"* (*Summa Theologiae*, I, q.22, a.3).

Creation and Fall

Creation is the special act by which God freely creates all things that exist out of nothing. The Fall is the historical event of the first parents of the human race freely choosing to disobey God and suffering serious consequences for themselves and all subsequent generations.

Do I need to believe that the world was created in seven days to be a good Catholic?

No, I do not need to believe that the world was created in seven literal days to be a good Catholic. In fact, St Augustine, as early as the fifth century, argued that the 'days' of the account of creation in Genesis cannot mean literal days as measured by sunrise or sunset, since Genesis itself states that the sun was not made until the fourth 'day' (*City of God*, XI, 7). Scripture therefore shows that what is expressed by the word 'day', like much in Genesis, is a truth expressed by a metaphor or figure. One does not, therefore, need to believe (and Scripture might even suggest that one should *not* believe) that the world was created in seven literal days.

Why are the accounts of the creation and Fall in the book of Genesis relevant to us today if these are just ancient myths?

The accounts of the creation and Fall presented in Genesis are not ancient myths, if by 'myth' is meant something that is invented and untrue. Gen 1-2 reveals certain essential truths about God, creation and human beings by means of a revealed symbolic history. An example of such an essential truth revealed in Genesis is that there is just one true God, not several gods. Genesis also reveals that creation was originally good prior to the coming of evil, and that human beings, created in a distinct act, have a special relationship to God within creation "*Let us make humankind in our image, after our likeness*" (Gen 1:26).

The accounts of the creation and Fall also have important implications for subsequent moral decisions in all ages. Since human beings have been given a special dignity and intimate relationship to God, Genesis gives an important warning against the temptation to misuse human beings in any way. The account of the Fall also provides a strong warning about the attraction of evil, the possibility of seduction into evil and the consequent separation from God brought about by mortal sin.

Does the Big Bang theory contradict the Catholic faith in some way?

No, the Big Bang theory does not contradict the Catholic faith. Indeed, it was a Catholic priest, Fr Georges Lemaître, who first proposed this theory of universal expansion from a primitive, compact and fiery state. This priest was given great honours by the Church, becoming president of the Pontifical Academy of Science in 1936 and a prelate (Monsignor) in 1960. Such honours show that the Church does not consider that the Big Bang contradicts the Catholic faith.

Furthermore, while the Big Bang theory has now won widespread acceptance, it is often forgotten that there was considerable opposition to this theory for over thirty years.

Indeed, the Big Bang was often more popular with prominent persons within the Church, including Pope Pius XII, than many scientists outside the Church, such as the astronomer Sir Fred Hoyle. In the officially atheist Soviet Union as late as 1948, astronomers agreed to fight against Lemaître's theory, which they attacked as 'reactionary' and 'helping clericalism'.

Underlying the opposition of many atheists to the Big Bang theory was the sense that this theory, while not of itself proving the doctrine of creation, is intuitively harmonious with creation 'out of nothing', beginning with light (cf. Gen 1:3).

Does the theory of evolution contradict the Catholic faith in some way?

No, the theory of evolution does not necessarily contradict the Catholic faith. Indeed, the theory of genetics, which is closely associated with evolution today, was founded by a Catholic priest and Augustinian monk, Fr Gregor Mendel.

Nevertheless, while the human body may have evolved, the Church rejects any view that a human being is merely an animal, or that human morality should be guided by Darwinian principles (popularly expressed as 'survival of the fittest'). By contrast, the Catholic faith holds that we have souls, created directly by God to enable us to know and love him, by grace, as his adopted children. Furthermore, our greatest vocation is not the propagation of our genes, but to learn to love with God and as God loves and to be happy with him forever in heaven.

Further reading. *Compendium* questions 51-78; *Catechism* ccc. 279-421 covering: (i) the Creator (ccc. 279-324); (ii) heaven and earth (ccc. 325-354); man (ccc. 355-384); the Fall (ccc. 385-421).

Fragment of a stele with the inscription 'Beit David' ('House of David'), dating from the 9th century before Christ, discovered in Tel Dan, Israel, in 1993.

The scholarly consensus among archaeologists is that this fragment is an authentic reference to the Biblical King David, confirming his existence as a genuine person of history, not a figure of pious fiction.

Salvation History

CREED

Salvation history is the progressive unfolding of God's plan to save the human race from sin and death after the Fall. This plan gives the true meaning to the entire history of the world.

Many of the Old Testament stories seem rather incredible, like Eve being created from Adam's rib or Jonah being swallowed by a whale. How should we regard these stories?

The Old Testament contains many kinds of literature, some of which is history and some of which might be regarded as parables, rather as Jesus tells parables in the New Testament. In addition, a text from the Old Testament can often include a mixture of history and symbolism. With regard to what is clearly presented as history, such as the life of King David, there have been some dramatic archaeological discoveries in recent decades (*see opposite*). With regard to other texts, what can appear to be an incredible fable often has great spiritual significance. For example, Eve's creation from the rib of Adam (Gn 2:21-25) foreshadows the piercing of Christ's side with a lance (Jn 19:34), from which flowed blood and water: this event symbolises the sacramental birth of the Church, the bride of Christ. Similarly, Jonah being swallowed by a whale prefigures Christ being laid in the tomb for three days (Mt 12:40). These stories are an integral part of the Old Testament, by which God gives us a deeper insight into central Christian truths.

Why did God choose one people, the Jewish people, in the Old Testament, but in the New Testament wants everyone to be saved?

God chose one people in the Old Testament precisely because he willed to offer salvation to everyone. The vocation of the Jewish people in the Old Testament was to be purified and prepared for the birth of the incarnate Son of God, Jesus Christ, born as a Jew from a Jewish mother, who offered his life for the salvation of the whole world. Much of Jewish history in the Old Testament makes sense in the light of this preparation, a vocation which was a great privilege but which also involved great suffering and persecution.

Why does morality often appear different in the Old Testament? Why, for example, was adultery punished by death, divorce tolerated and why were certain pagan peoples killed?

These are some of many difficult moral challenges regarding aspects of the Old Testament, which is one reason why the Old Testament has to be interpreted, not in isolation, but with reference to the rest of Scripture and Tradition.

From the Christian perspective, one response is to say that, in the long path of salvation history, different stages required different emphases. In primitive times, pagan beliefs often resembled a kind of chaotic spiritual jungle, both morally and intellectually (rather like New Age and spiritualist beliefs today). God needed the Jewish people to separate themselves clearly from this jungle, which would otherwise have choked and obliterated the ground being prepared for the coming of

Christ. Hence there were strong commandments against idolatry in the Old Testament and wars against certain pagan peoples in Canaan and the surrounding area. Another response is to say that many Old Testament laws and practices were provisional, offsetting the worst effects of sin, but being superseded with the coming of Christ. So, for example, Jesus says that divorce was tolerated by Moses, not because this was God's original intention regarding marriage, but because the people's hearts were 'hardened' (Mk 10:5). Yet another response is to say that the harsh laws in the Old Testament, such as death for adultery, help to teach us about the seriousness of sin. When the scribes and Pharisees bring a woman to Jesus who has committed adultery, he does not contradict the Old Testament. What he says is, "*Let him who is without sin among you be the first to throw a stone at her*," and then, "*Go, and do not sin again*"(John 8:7, 11). The Old Testament teaches us about the seriousness of sin and helps to highlight what is radically new about Christianity: through Jesus Christ, our sins can be forgiven and we can be reconciled with God.

Finally, when reading Scripture, it must also be remembered that death, although a great evil, is not the worst evil that can befall a person. Indeed, Christianity, even after the revelation of the New Testament, recognises the legitimacy of war in extreme cases. The worst evil that can befall a person is to lose heaven. If, as has been observed, we write the 'title page' in this life of what we are to be in eternity, it is not how long we live, but our relationship to God that truly matters.

Further reading. *Compendium* questions 6-8 and 102; *Catechism* ccc. 50-64 covering: (i) revelation (ccc. 50-53); (ii) the stages of revelation (ccc. 54-64).

Rylands Papyrus 457 (P52)

The oldest known papyrus fragment of the New Testament, dating from c. 125 – 150 AD. This fragment was discovered in Egypt in 1920 and is now at the John Rylands Library in Manchester. The text corresponds to John 18:31-33, part of the account of the trial of Jesus. Another discovery from the last century, the Dead Sea Scrolls, has been important in validating the Septuagint, the Greek version of the Hebrew Scriptures widely used by early Christians.

The Incarnation

> By the word 'Incarnation' we mean that God the Son took to himself a human nature for the sake of our salvation.

Does the Bible actually say that Jesus is God and that he claimed to be God?

Yes, the Bible says explicitly that Jesus is God. An example of such a statement is when St Thomas says to the risen Jesus, *"My Lord and my God"* (Jn 20:28). The Bible also records instances in which Jesus confirmed his divinity in response to statements or questions about his identity asked by others. When asked the following question directly by the high priest, *"Are you the Christ, the Son of the Blessed?"* Jesus responded, *"I am"* (Mk 14:61-62; cf. Mt 26:63-64). Furthermore, the fact that Jesus was then condemned to death for blasphemy shows that his listeners had understood his claim to be divine.

The deeper mystery in Scripture, however, is not whether Jesus is divine but the sense in which he is divine. In the Gospels, Jesus generally refers to himself as the 'Son' or the 'beloved Son', and he is also described as the 'Son of God' (cf. Mt 27:54, Mk 14:33, Lk 1:35, Jn 3:18). This phrase, 'Son of God', is not some honorific phrase, as St John and Hebrews show when they speak of Jesus as the *only and uniquely begotten Son* (Jn 1:14; Heb 1:5). The implication of this uniqueness is that Jesus is not an adopted or honorific 'son of God' or a different 'god' from his heavenly Father. On the contrary, Jesus has the 'fullness of God' (Col 1:19), describing himself as being 'one' with his heavenly Father (Jn 10:30). In other words, whatever can be attributed to God as God can be attributed correctly to Jesus Christ. Scripture further confirms this truth by reporting occasions on which Jesus is not only honoured but worshipped (cf. Mt 2:1, Mt 14:33, Jn 9:38). Scripture also affirms that Jesus has the power to forgive sins (cf. Mk 2:1-12), an ability attributed uniquely to God by those listening. Finally, Jesus asserted his eternal existence and divinity by saying that he existed before Abraham and by applying to himself the name of God revealed to Moses, *"Before Abraham was, I AM"* (Jn 8:58, cf. Ex 3:14). By attempting, after these words, to stone Jesus to death for blasphemy, his listeners showed they had understood his meaning, *"It is not for a good work that we stone you but for blasphemy; because you, being a man, make yourself God."* (Jn 10:33). Therefore, the Bible does say that Jesus is God – the only begotten Son of God, that he substantiated this claim by his words and deeds, and that his listeners understood his claim.

Did the Church invent Jesus' divinity centuries after his death?

All the relevant historical documents show that belief in the divinity of Christ was central to the faith of the first Christians and not something invented by the Church centuries later. First, much of the New Testament was written well before the end of the first century by the apostles or those closely associated with them. Since the New Testament affirms Jesus' divinity, as argued above, the first Christians to have known Jesus personally clearly believed in his divinity. Second, other early documents confirm the consistency of early Christian belief in the divinity of Christ. For example, St Ignatius wrote in c. 107 AD, "*Our God, Jesus Christ, was conceived by Mary in accord with God's plan: of the seed of David, it is true, but also of the Holy Spirit*" (*Letter to the Ephesians*, 18:2). Since, in this letter, St Ignatius explicitly describes Jesus Christ as 'our God', it is clear that early Christians recognised Christ's divinity. Finally, the pagan historian Pliny the Younger informed the Emperor Trajan at the beginning of the second century that Christians regularly met to worship Christ 'as a god' (*Letters* 10.96). Although Pliny did not fully understand Christianity, his letter confirms that the early Christians *worshipped* Christ as divine, rather than honouring him merely as a great man or prophet.

Do some early texts about Christ, such as the 'gnostic gospels', deny his divinity?

Contrary to popular belief, the so-called 'gnostic gospels' do not deny the divinity of Christ. On the contrary, these false gospels tend to downplay the humanity of Christ. In the so-called *Infancy Gospel of Thomas*, for example, the child 'Jesus' is depicted as rather alien and malevolent, hurting and killing people by divine power when they disturb him (3 – 5).

Furthermore, even the earliest texts of these gnostic gospels come from the later second century, well after the completion of the books of the New Testament. The gnostic gospels are not, therefore, a reliable guide to the beliefs of the first Christians but belong, rather, to attempts in subsequent centuries to subvert early Christian belief.

Further reading. *Compendium* questions 79-104; *Catechism* ccc. 422-486, especially (i) the titles of Jesus Christ (ccc. 430-455); (ii) true and false beliefs about the Incarnation (ccc. 461-483).

The Pilate Stone

This block of limestone, discovered in 1961, has a carved inscription referring to Pontius Pilate, who condemned Jesus Christ to scourging and death by crucifixion c. 33. The second and third lines of reconstructed text read, *"Pontius Pilate, the prefect of Judaea,"* affirming Pilate's existence and office.

The Life of Christ

The life of Christ is the life that the incarnate Son of God lived upon earth from the time of his conception until his Ascension.

Did Jesus Christ really exist?

Yes, Jesus Christ really existed. The life and work of Jesus Christ are probably better attested than our knowledge of any other person in the ancient world. We know about Jesus Christ principally by means of the twenty-seven documents known as the New Testament. These constitute the largest volume of written evidence in the ancient world about any one person. Other early Christian works corroborate many details of Jesus' life. Furthermore, records made by the two greatest non-Christian historians of this period affirm some basic facts about Jesus: the Roman historian Tacitus confirms that Christ suffered the 'extreme penalty' under Pontius Pilate; the Jewish historian Josephus refers to Jesus who was called 'the Christ' and to his trial by the Sanhedrin.

Are the Gospel accounts of the life of Jesus Christ accurate?

The gospels themselves emphasise that they are accounts drawn from the testimony of eyewitnesses, implying both the desire and the means to draw up accurate accounts of the life of Christ. The Gospel of John, for example, states, *"He who saw it has borne witness – his testimony is true, and he knows that he*

23

tells the truth – that you also may believe" (John 19:35). The gospel of Luke also begins by stating that the account is taken from eyewitnesses, in other words, people who had known Jesus personally during his public ministry and after his Resurrection. Furthermore, writing in the second century, St Irenaeus confirms that the gospels were written by those intimately associated with Jesus or his apostles, "*Matthew also issued a written Gospel among the Hebrews in their own dialect, while Peter and Paul were preaching at Rome, and laying the foundations of the Church. After their departure, Mark, the disciple and interpreter of Peter, did also hand down to us in writing what had been preached by Peter. Luke also, the companion of Paul, recorded in a book the Gospel preached by him. Afterwards, John, the disciple of the Lord, who also had leaned upon His breast, did himself publish a Gospel during his residence at Ephesus in Asia*" (*Adversus Haereses*, III.1, c. 180 AD). As to whether the gospels were written in good faith, it is hard to see any motive for the authors writing what they did not believe about Christ, especially as their love for Christ brought the apostles persecution and even death.

Were the gospel accounts of the life of Jesus Christ modified in later centuries?

Evidence for the textual stability of the gospels is that many early Christian writers cite substantially and extensively the same texts that we use today. To give one example, St Justin Martyr in his *Dialogue with Trypho*, written in the middle of the second century, cites the words of John the Baptist and Jesus in those verses now classified as Mt 3:11-12 and Mt 17:12, "*... 'I baptise you with water ... He shall baptise you with the Holy Spirit and with fire'...etc*" (*Dialogue*, 49). To give another example, Tertullian, at the start of the third century, cites passages from the four gospels, Acts, Epistles of Paul, I Peter, I John, Jude and Revelation. Furthermore, early papyrus fragments of New Testament texts have been discovered which have been matched to texts of the canon as it is known to us today (an example being the Rylands Papyrus 457 [P52] shown on p.19). Finally, two large physical manuscripts have survived from the fourth century that together cover nearly the entire New Testament, the *Codex Vaticanus* and the *Codex Sinaiticus*. The cumulative effect of all these sources, together with intensive work in textual criticism over the past two centuries, gives us a high degree of confidence in the substantial integrity of the New Testament texts we have today.

Why can't we say that Jesus Christ was simply a good man or moral teacher?

Given his claims to be the Son of God, we cannot simply say that Jesus was a good man or moral teacher. As C.S. Lewis said, *"A man who was merely a man and said the sort of things Jesus said would not be a great moral teacher. He would either be a lunatic -on a level with the man who says he is a poached egg- or else he would be the Devil of Hell. You must make your choice. Either this man was, and is, the Son of God; or else a madman or something worse"* (Mere Christianity, III). In other words, there are only three possible conclusions that we can reach regarding Jesus Christ: either he was mad or he was bad or he was God himself come to save us. He cannot simply be a good man or moral teacher.

Further reading. *Compendium* questions 105-111; *Catechism* ccc. 512-570, especially the mysteries of: (i) Jesus' infancy and hidden life (ccc. 522-534); (ii) Jesus' public life (ccc. 535-570).

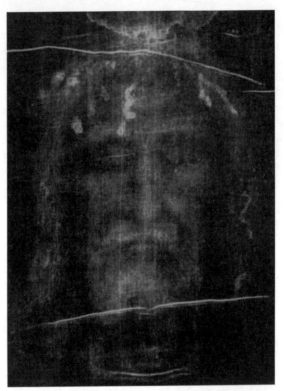

A photographic negative of the face of the Shroud of Turin

The Shroud of Turin is a linen cloth bearing the image of a man who appears wounded in a manner consistent with scourging and crucifixion. The shroud has attracted great interest since the discovery in 1898 that the image appears clearer as a photographic negative. Despite intense scientific investigation, it has proved surprisingly difficult to discover the origin of the shroud image. The Church has neither endorsed or rejected the shroud as genuine, but has approved its association with devotion to the Holy Face of Jesus.

The Paschal Mystery

CREED

> The Paschal mystery is the Passion, death and Resurrection of Jesus Christ by which he heals us from sin and enables us to become children of God.

How does Jesus' death save us from our sins?

Scripture and Tradition are clear that Jesus' death sacrificial death has ransomed us from sin and reconciled us to God. As St Peter says, *"You know that you were ransomed ... with the precious blood of Christ"* (1 Pet 1:18). Scripture also assures us of the many fruits of Christ's sacrifice. By means of his sacrifice, Jesus has: repaid our debt of guilt (Mt 20:28); gained mercy for us and repealed our punishment (Mt 26:28); defeated the claims of the devil over us (Jn 12:31); reconciled us to God (2 Cor 5:19); and fulfilled Scripture and salvation history (Col 1:20).

Exactly how Jesus' death has produced such fruitfulness does remain something of a mystery. Indeed, a complete answer to this question may well be beyond our comprehension. What we do know, however, is that on the cross, Jesus suffered the effects of sin for us, his divine love revoking the offence of all sins and bearing the pain and cost of sin in itself. The key words are 'love' and 'sacrifice': it is a mistake to think of Christ's death in cold and calculating terms, as if an angry God needed someone to suffer to placate his wrath. It is more truthful to say that, united with us out of love, Christ took our sins upon himself that we might live.

Was salvation possible for those who lived before Christ's sacrifice on Calvary?

Yes, salvation was possible for those who lived before Christ's sacrificial death. In fact, Jesus names certain souls, namely Abraham, Isaac, Jacob and all the prophets, as being among those who would sit at table in the kingdom of heaven (Mt 8:11; Lk 13:28). All these persons had some connection with Christ, insofar as their words and actions witnessed to his future coming. Nevertheless, it is generally believed that these just souls could not enter heaven before Christ's descent to free them from their place of waiting (cf. 1 Pet 3:18-2; Mt 27:51-53).

Why did Jesus, after the Resurrection, only appear to certain witnesses, and what evidence is available for all those of us who are not in this privileged group?

Although Jesus only appeared to certain witnesses after the Resurrection, the number and variety of witnesses gives a secure foundation for belief on the basis of testimonial evidence. Indeed, St Paul records that Jesus had appeared to several hundred people (1 Cor 15:6). There is not one instance of any of these witnesses to the risen Jesus denying the Resurrection later, even in the face of persecution and death.

Those of us who are not in this group rely on these witnesses, whose lives were fruitful in proclaiming the truth of the Resurrection and whose words and actions are recorded in the New Testament. Nevertheless, while it might appear that these chosen witnesses to the Resurrection were specially privileged, Jesus says that it is those have not seen and yet believe who are blessed (John 20:29). As with much of Revelation, God reveals himself in a way that invites us to believe rather than compels belief, allowing us freedom to accept him or reject him.

With regard to the Resurrection, two other points should be noted. First, no definitive proof can be offered against the Resurrection, since the tomb in which Jesus had been laid after his crucifixion was found to be empty on the third day, despite being under a Roman guard (Mt 27:66). Second, certain physical signs in the world today may bear witness, indirectly, to the truth of the Resurrection. In particular, the bodies of some of the saints, such as St Bernadette, have not decayed in the normal way and remain in good condition for decades or even centuries (cf. Acts 2:27). While the souls of these saints are in heaven, the preservation of their bodies from normal decay can be interpreted as a foreshadowing or prophecy of the final Resurrection from the dead at the end of time.

Does Christ's Ascension mean that the Bible implies heaven to be above our heads?

No. The Ascension shows us the freedom of the Resurrected body and was a visible sign of Jesus' entering heaven in his glorified human nature; Christ's Ascension is not intended to teach us that heaven is literally above our heads.

Further reading. *Compendium* questions 112-132; *Catechism* ccc. 571-667, especially: (i) Christ's redemptive death in God's plan of salvation (ccc. 599-605); (ii) Christ's offering of himself to the Father for our sins (ccc. 606-623); (iii) Christ's descent into hell (ccc. 632-637); (iv) his rising from the dead (ccc. 638-658); (v) his Ascension into heaven (ccc. 659-667).

The Holy Trinity with Mary Magdalene, St John the Baptist and Tobias and the Angel
by Alessandro Botticelli

The variety of images of the Trinity emphasise distinct but complementary aspects of the Godhead. In Botticelli's picture above, the emphasis is on the revelation of the Trinity through Jesus Christ. The Father, for example, is depicted as older than the Son not because the Father is literally older, but to emphasise the relationship of the Father to the Son who has revealed Him.

The Trinity

The Trinity is the one God in three persons,
Father, Son and Holy Spirit.

What is the best way to represent or think of the Trinity?

No one representation of the Trinity could ever be adequate to express every aspect of the Trinity, which exceeds any created thing. So the best way to represent the Trinity is to try to avoid just one, single image, but to use a variety of images to emphasise distinct but complementary aspects of the Godhead. Certain images are good at emphasising the unity of the Godhead. An example of such an image is the Irish Shamrock, a single plant with three leaves, which was used by St Patrick when preaching the gospel to the pagan tribes of Ireland in the fifth century. A second group of images emphasise better the distinction of the divine persons, a famous example being Andrei Rublev's icon. The equality of the figures in this icon shows that they are the one God, but the gaze of their eyes, their clothing and the background objects distinguish their relationships. A third group of images emphasise the revelation of the Trinity through Jesus Christ. An example from this last category is the image by Alessandro Botticelli (*see opposite*). Note how this painting depicts the Father as being older and with a beard, not because God the Father is literally older than God the Son (which would make no sense) but to highlight the relationship of the Father to the Son who has revealed Him. Similarly, the Spirit is represented as a dove between the Father and the Son, indicating how the Spirit proceeds from the Father and the Son and unites the Father and the Son. Such diverse representations of the Trinity are helpful provided we grasp what they show and in what ways they remain limited.

How can God be both three and one at the same time? That doesn't make sense!

That which is three in one sense can, at the same time, be one in another sense without being contradictory. For example, the three sides of a triangle are three insofar as they are sides, but are inseparably one insofar as they are a triangle. So while the Trinity undoubtedly exceeds human comprehension, the teaching about the Trinity that has been drawn from revelation, namely that God is 'one substance, three persons', is not, in itself, inherently contradictory.

What is the practical impact of the Trinity on our lives?

Since the Trinity is the central revelation of Christianity about God, the practical impact of the Trinity is intimately linked to every aspect of our lives as Christians. To select one example, the revelation that God is a Trinity (rather than, for example, God as a singular person, if this were possible) underlines the foundational importance of interpersonal relationships comprising two key elements: a perfect unity of love, yet without one person absorbing the others or annihilating their personal identity. These principles are reflected, for example, in the institution of Christian marriage, the notion of Christian friendship and a vision of society in which properly distinct institutions work in mutual harmony. One related idea is the Catholic political principle of *subsidiarity*. Another practical impact of the Trinity on our lives is that this revelation can give us hope for our future happiness in heaven. In particular, the revealed life of the Trinity answers two deep and conflicting human fears – loneliness and loss of identity. Just as the persons of the Trinity are united but distinct in their communion, in heaven we shall be neither isolated nor absorbed. Indeed, in relationship with God in heaven we shall also truly be ourselves and know ourselves.

To which of the divine persons should our prayers be addressed?

We may address prayers to the Holy Trinity or to any person of the Holy Trinity, but some prayers are most fittingly addressed to one of the divine persons. In liturgical prayer, for example, in which we participate in the action of Christ as high priest, we generally address prayers *to* the Father, *through* the Son and *in the unity of* the Holy Spirit. Prayers for God's mercy, especially to the Sacred Heart, are often addressed to the Son, while in praying for the gifts of the Holy Spirit or for the fire of divine love, we generally address the Holy Spirit.

Further reading. *Compendium* questions 33-50 and 136-146; *Catechism* ccc. 199-267 and ccc. 683-747, especially: (i) belief in God (ccc. 199-231); (ii) the revelation of God as Trinity (ccc. 238-248); (iii) the Holy Trinity in the teaching of the faith (ccc. 249-256); (iv) the divine works and Trinitarian missions (ccc. 257-260); (v) belief in the Holy Spirit (ccc. 683-686).

*The tomb of St Peter under the main altar and the dome of
St Peter's Basilica in Rome*

Jesus said to St Peter, *"You are Peter, and on this rock I will build my church, and the
powers of death shall not prevail against it"* (Mt 16:18). This prophecy of Jesus has
been fulfilled by the office of St Peter, held by successive Popes, which has
proved to be a firm foundation for the Catholic Church since the time of the
apostles. The construction of St Peter's basilica above the apostle's tomb is a
physical symbol of the foundation of the Church on the rock of Peter.

The Church

The Church is the mystical body of Christ, established by God on earth to gather humanity to divine life in heaven.

Can I be a Christian without being a member of the Church?

To live as a Christian in the full and proper sense means being a member of the Church. After all, Christ himself taught that he would build one Church – his Church – 'on the rock of Peter' (Mt 16:18), and that a Christian should 'listen to the Church' (Mt 18:17). In other words, Christ did not intend his followers to be isolated individuals or members of a patchwork of disunited communities. In addition, the New Testament strongly emphasises the centrality of the Church to the Christian life. St Paul claims that the Church is the 'body of Christ' (Eph 5:23), even describing their union like that of a husband and wife. This love between Christ and his Church is so strong that Christ regards persecution of his Church as persecution of himself (Acts 9:4; 22:7; 26:14). St Paul also describes the exclusion of an unrepentant sinner from the Church community as being 'handed over to Satan' (1 Tim 1:20; 1 Cor 5:5), implying that separation from the Church puts one's soul at risk. Christian saints in later centuries also emphasised the importance of the Church. St Cyprian, a bishop and martyr in the third century, wrote, *"He cannot have God for his father, who has not the Church for his mother"* (Treatise on Unity, 6).

So while one can be Christian without being in full communion with the Church, such a state is unsatisfactory. This condition of being separated from the Church is only sinful, however, when one is cut off from the Church due to one's own fault.

How do I know that the Catholic Church today is the same Church founded by Christ?

The main way in which we know that the Catholic Church today is the Church founded by Jesus Christ is the continuity of the Church since the time of the apostles. This claim does not imply an assertion that the Catholic Church today exactly resembles that of the early Christians, but that the Catholic Church today has developed in a continuous manner from the early Church. This development has an organic coherence, like that of a plant growing from a seed.

This coherence and continuity of the Church through history can be seen, first, from the way that even early Christian writings refer to the 'Catholic Church', the word 'catholic' (*katholikos*), meaning 'universal', 'complete' and 'whole'. In approximately 107 AD, for example, St Ignatius, who was bishop of Antioch, wrote, *"Wherever the bishop appears, there let the people be; as wherever Jesus Christ is, there is the Catholic Church"* (*Letter to the Smyrnaeans*, 8). St Ignatius, who links the presence of Jesus Christ to the Catholic Church in this text, refers elsewhere to the Church in Rome as 'presiding' over love. A second mark of continuity is the structure of Holy Orders: St Ignatius also refers to bishops, priests and deacons, essentially the same structure of Holy Orders that exists in the Catholic Church today. Furthermore, the office of Bishop of Rome, who is usually referred to today as the Pope, is not a modern invention but can also be traced back to the early Church. In

Scripture, Peter is singled out as having a special role among all the apostles (cf. Mt 16:18) and early Church writings emphasise the continuation of this office by his successors. In 180 AD, St Irenaeus records that the Church of Rome had maintained a perpetual succession of bishops from the time of its founding by the apostles Peter and Paul and that it is essential for every local church to be united with the Church of Rome, on account of its 'pre-eminent authority' (*Against Heresies*, III.3). Uniquely in the world today, however, only the Catholic Church still maintains this communion with the Bishop of Rome. By contrast, the vast majority of the other Christian communities today, now numbering many thousands, tend to fragment easily and are generally much less than five centuries old. So notwithstanding the many moral and other imperfections of her individual members, there is, therefore, a unique, organic continuity between the Catholic Church today and the Church of the early Christians.

In the nineteenth century, John Henry Newman developed detailed arguments that identified the Roman Catholic Church with the early Christian Church, a conclusion that eventually led Newman himself to be received into the Catholic Church. His *Apologia Pro Vita Sua* and *Lectures on Certain Difficulties Felt by Anglicans* may be helpful to those who wish to explore the historical and theological issues in detail.

Further reading. *Compendium* questions 147-195; *Catechism* ccc. 748-962, especially: (i) the Church's origin, foundation and mission (ccc. 758-769); (ii) the mystery of the Church (ccc. 770-780); (iii) the Church as one, holy, catholic and apostolic (ccc. 811-870); (iv) the hierarchy, laity and consecrated life (ccc. 871-945); (v) the communion of saints (ccc. 946-962).

The Venerable John Henry Cardinal Newman

Newman argued that Tradition unfolds over time, drawing out consequences from Revelation that were not obvious at earlier times. He converted to Catholicism from Anglicanism in 1845 when he had become convinced that the Catholic Church was in unique continuity with the early Church.

Scripture and Tradition

> Scripture and Tradition together constitute the single deposit of revealed truth given by God to the Church and infallibly taught by the Magisterium.

Can't the Bible alone teach us everything we need to know about revelation?

Although the Bible is the entire content of God's inspired written truth, it does not follow that the Bible alone can teach us everything we need to know about revelation. First, the Bible is a difficult book requiring careful interpretation, especially as many truths are expressed as parables or signs. Second, even an infallible text, when interpreted by imperfect individuals, can be used to justify all kinds of wrong ideas.

The fact that the Bible alone is insufficient is also shown by the painful lesson of Christian history, especially during the past five centuries. The Protestant movement, initiated by the actions of Martin Luther in 1517, advocated the principle that the Bible alone (*sola Scriptura*) is sufficient for us to know everything about revelation. In principle, therefore, all Protestants, by relying on this one text, should be united in their faith. Yet in practice, Protestantism is extremely disunited and has continually fragmented throughout its history. No one knows precisely how many Protestant ecclesial bodies exist today, but the number is estimated between 8,000 and 30,000. Furthermore, these congregations differ, not just in minor matters, but also in regard to some of the most central matters of Christianity, even disagreeing about the divinity of Christ and the means of salvation.

As the early Christians realised when faced with various doctrinal controversies, it is necessary to appeal to the oral tradition passed down from the apostles and to have a final, infallible authority to adjudicate among interpretations of Scripture. Furthermore, early Christians realised that God has blessed us with such an authority in the teaching office of the Church. While Scripture itself does not support the Protestant claim that Scripture *alone* is sufficient, it does tell us that the Church is *"the pillar and bulwark of the truth"* (1 Tim 3:15).

How do we know that the books that were included in the Bible are the right ones?

We know that the seventy-three books of the Bible are the right ones by the authority of the Catholic Church and because these books have been regarded as inspired since the early Church. As St Augustine wrote, *"I would not believe in the Gospel, had not the authority of the Catholic Church already moved me"* Contra Epistolam Manichaei 5, 6 (ccc. 119), in other words, the living authority of the Church validates these books as Scripture. Such a claim does not mean that the 'canon' (the list of books recognised as Scripture) was complete and clear-cut at the very beginning of Christianity, not least because the books themselves were still being written in the first century. What is clear is that the two central sets of New Testament books, the Gospels and Epistles of St Paul, were quickly accorded a special status by the Church, being cited by early Christian writers such as St Ignatius, St Clement of Rome and St Polycarp. From other sources, especially the writings of St

Irenaeus and a manuscript called the *Muratorian Fragment* (c. 170 AD), we also know that the Church, by the end of the second century, accepted most of the remaining books of the present New Testament as Scripture. The early Church also recognised the Jewish Scriptures written before the coming of Christ as the divinely inspired 'Old Testament'. The oldest complete manuscript of the Bible, the 4th century *Codex Vaticanus*, confirms that the Church included in this Old Testament certain later Jewish works written in Greek, texts that are also cited by New Testament writers. These Greek works are: Tobit, Judith, 1 and 2 Maccabees, the Wisdom of Solomon, Sirach (Ecclesiasticus), Baruch and additional parts of Daniel and Esther. From Luther's time, however, Protestantism has not recognised these works as canonical.

How can the Magisterium teach infallibly when there have been some evil popes?

The answer to this question is foreshadowed by Jesus' words about the scribes and Pharisees, *"Practice and observe whatever they tell you, but not what they do; for they preach, but do not practice"* (Mt 23:3). God has given the teaching office of the Church protection from error, to ensure that people in every age will have access to the gospel of salvation. Fortunately, however, this protection does not depend on the moral quality of the Pope and bishops in communion with him, even though the Church suffers greatly if its shepherds are corrupt.

Further reading. *Compendium* questions 6-24; *Catechism* ccc. 74-141, especially the: (i) Apostolic Tradition (ccc. 75-79); (ii) relationship of Tradition and Scripture (ccc. 80-83); (iii) interpretation of the heritage of faith (ccc. 84-100); Sacred Scripture (ccc. 101-141).

A picture of the original image of Our Lady of Guadalupe,
patroness of the Americas and protector of the unborn.

The image of Our Lady of Guadalupe is believed to be of miraculous origin,
containing clear references to Rev 12:1. The Church believes that miracles are
not unique to Biblical times, but that God continues to work miracles in
support of the work of salvation. The process of canonisation, that is, the
recognition that a person is a saint in heaven, usually requires evidence that
the intercession of that person has brought about at least two miracles.

Mary and the Four Last Things

CREED

Mary was conceived immaculate. As a virgin, she became Mother of God by bearing Jesus. She was without sin, assumed body and soul into heaven, and is the Mother of the Church.

Do Catholics worship Mary as divine?

No, Catholics honour and love Mary as the Mother of God and our heavenly mother, as well as praying for her powerful intercession, but do not worship her as divine (cf. Rev. 19:10).

Scripture doesn't seem to require us to have a devotion to Mary. Isn't such devotion a recent embellishment or even corruption of the ancient and pure Christian faith?

On the contrary, Scripture does, in fact, imply that devotion to Mary is fitting and fruitful for Christians. For example, the *Hail Mary*, the most famous devotional prayer to Mary, repeats the words that Elizabeth uses in the Gospel of Luke, "*Blessed art thou among women*" (Lk 1:42) Furthermore, those who say these words in prayer fulfil an important Scriptural prophecy of Mary, "*Henceforth all generations will call me blessed*" (Lk 1:48). In addition, just as the Ark of the Covenant, which bore the word of God on tablets of stone, was fittingly honoured in the Old Testament, it is even more important for Christians to honour Mary, who bore the Word made flesh.

Furthermore, devotion to Mary is not a novelty or corruption of the ancient Christian faith. As early as the second century, St Irenaeus referred to Mary as the 'second Eve' and an 'advocate' (*Against Heresies*, V.19) and the Council of Ephesus in 431 AD defended the ancient title of Mary as the 'Mother of God'. Furthermore, a Rylands Library papyrus records a mid-third century hymn to Mary now known as the *Sub Tuum Praesidium*, "*Under your mercy we take refuge, O Mother of God. Do not reject our supplications in necessity, but deliver us from danger, [O you] alone pure and alone blessed.*" These sources give clear evidence of a special devotion to Mary in the early Church.

What are the benefits of prayers to Mary and the saints? Isn't Christ sufficient for us?

Christ is certainly sufficient for us in the sense that he has the power and the will to give us everything that we need for our salvation. Nevertheless, Scripture also teaches us that God often wants to help us when others pray to him on our behalf, underlining the importance of intercession by those who are close to him. In the Old Testament, for example, it is the intercession of Moses that secures the forgiveness of the Israelites when they worship a golden calf (Ex 32). In the New Testament, St Stephen intercedes for the men stoning him to death (Acts 7:60). One of those present at his execution later converts to the Christian faith, becoming the great St Paul.

Furthermore, the New Testament draws special attention to the power of Mary's intercession with God. John records that it is at Mary's request (Jn 2:3) that Jesus works his first miracle, turning water into wine. Now that Mary and the other saints enjoy the vision of God, their prayers as our intercessors are even more beneficial in the cause of our salvation.

Eternal happiness in heaven seems fine, but how could a God of love, or indeed a God of justice, consign anyone to hell – forever?

Some general principles can help us understand this difficult teaching. First, Scripture is clear that God loves us beyond all comprehension, even to the extent of becoming a man and dying for us. Second, Scripture is also clear that God desires all people to be saved (1 Tim 2:4) and to be with him forever in heaven. To enter hell, therefore, can only be the outcome of human choices that are opposed to God's will. Third, the human soul cannot continue in a state of flux forever, sometimes surrendering to God's grace and sometimes becoming hardened against grace. Such a fate would condemn everyone, saints and sinners alike, to an unending, restless eternity. So God, in his mercy, brings every life to a conclusion that is permanent, and not subject to further change. Fourth, Jesus' parable about the last judgment (Mt 25:31-46), implies that the damned have no true love for God or anyone else. Lacking love, they would, therefore, be incapable of enjoying heaven and the communion of saints.

Finally, some authors, such as Dante, suggest that the damned do, in a sense, receive what they want. The problem is that what they want from God is something that entails being without God. Such a state is incompatible with happiness.

Further reading. *Compendium* questions 94-100, 133-135, 196-199 and 202-216; *Catechism* ccc. 963-1060 covering especially: (i) Mary as the mother of Christ (ccc. 963-975); (ii) Mary as the mother of the Church (ccc. 988-1060); (iii) the resurrection of the body (ccc. 988-1019); (iv) life everlasting (ccc. 1020-1060).

The Communion of the Apostles by Fra Angelico

Christian liturgy and sacraments were founded by Jesus Christ, who commanded his disciples, "*Do this in remembrance of me*" (Lk 22:19).

Liturgy and Sacraments

The sacred liturgy is the true worship of God, enacted by Jesus Christ and his body, the Church, through the power of the Holy Spirit. It is a shared 'public work' (*leitourgia*) with ceremonies, rites and formulas established by Scripture and Tradition. Sacraments are signs established by Christ that cause what they signify. The sacraments heal us from sin and plant, nourish or restore the life of grace in us.

Why is liturgy necessary when one can pray to God in many other ways?

The Church has liturgy in obedience to God, especially the explicit command of Jesus Christ when he instituted the Eucharist, "*Do this in remembrance of me*" (Lk 22:19). To pray to God in the liturgy does not, of course, preclude praying to God in many other ways, especially in personal prayer each day. Nevertheless, the liturgies of the Old Testament, which foreshadow the new covenant established by Christ, as well as the references to liturgies in the New Testament and the early Church, and the tradition of the last two thousand years makes it clear that liturgy is central to our prayer to God.

Why, then, is liturgy so important? One reason is that the Church is the 'Body of Christ' or the 'Bride of Christ'. In the liturgy we do not, therefore, pray merely as individuals but as members of this body on earth and in heaven. In order for this prayer of the Church to be harmonious, however, it is important that there are established words and actions to follow. Here the analogy of an orchestra may be helpful. If every musician decides to invent his or her own music, the overall result is nothing but noise. When, however, the musicians follow the score, the result can be music of profound richness and beauty. Similarly, the liturgy, by following words and actions drawn from revelation, frees us to contribute harmoniously to giving glory to God.

Why is it important to follow the liturgical forms received from Scripture and Tradition rather than, for example, inventing liturgical rites for ourselves?

One answer to this question is practical, namely that people would tend to disagree about what new forms any invented liturgy would take. The parable in Scripture that warns us of this risk is the story of the Tower of Babel (Gen 11:1-9), in which people try to build a tower to heaven and end up being unable to understand one another. A deeper answer is that those who invent new liturgies risk worshipping false gods. The Bible warns of this danger by the story of the golden calf (Exod 32), in which the Israelites broke their covenant with God by worshipping the image of a beast. So to ensure that we worship the true God, the form of all Catholic rites is drawn from Scripture, developed through Tradition and sanctioned by the Magisterium, the Church's teaching office.

Furthermore, the established liturgical rites provide many obvious spiritual benefits. First, these rites have nourished the lives of countless saints and embody the cumulative insight of centuries of Christian worship. Second, there is a clear wisdom in many of the words and actions of these rites. For example, it is one matter to accept that the body and blood of Christ are present on the altar, but liturgical actions such as genuflection, or the elevation of the host in the Mass, help to form an attitude of worship towards the Eucharist. In this and many other ways of which we may not be fully aware, the liturgy helps to prepare us for heaven, when we shall no longer see 'in a mirror dimly' (cf. 1 Cor 13:12), but face-to-face.

How do Catholic and Protestant beliefs differ with regard to the sacraments?

Sacraments are not central to Protestant forms of worship in the same way as they are in the Catholic Church. While the thousands of Protestant communities in the world today have very divergent views regarding the sacraments, they often consider that the sacraments do not cause the grace they signify, but are a kind of extrinsic sign of God's action.

In addition, most Protestants recognise just two sacraments, Baptism and the Eucharist, rather than seven. Regarding the Eucharist, Protestant beliefs (including the articles of the Church of England) usually deny transubstantiation, reject the worship of the Eucharist and oppose Catholic teaching that the Mass is a sacrifice. Since Protestantism denies that the Eucharist is a sacrifice, it also lacks a sacramental priesthood.

Further reading. *Compendium* questions 218-250; *Catechism* ccc. 1066-1209 covering especially: (i) the liturgy in general (ccc. 1066-1112); (ii) the sacraments in general (ccc. 1113-1134); (iii) the celebration of sacramental liturgy (ccc. 1135-1209).

*An early fourth century baptistery in the Byzantine Cathedral of Our Lady
in Paros, one of the oldest baptisteries in the world.*

The existence of ancient baptisteries, such as the one above, testifies to the
importance of Baptism to Christians of all times and places. Baptism is the
gateway to the whole Christian life. This ancient baptistery in Paros, designed
in the shape of a cross, also shows how early Christians understood Baptism
to be connected to the death and Resurrection of Jesus Christ.

Baptism and Confirmation

Baptism is the sacrament by which we become Christians. It frees us from Original Sin, makes us children of God, temples of the Holy Spirit and members of the Church.

Confirmation completes the Christian initiation begun in Baptism, making us spiritually adult by means of a permanent 'seal' upon our souls. In this sacrament the Holy Spirit also gives us seven gifts that enable us to see and act well spiritually. These gifts empower us to publicly proclaim the Gospel and to defend the faith against opposition.

If the Christian life begins with Baptism, what about those good people who are not Baptised? Are they without grace and, if so, are they destined for hell?

In the New Testament, Jesus describes the people living before the flood as "*eating and drinking, marrying and giving in marriage, until the day when Noah entered the ark.*" Now eating, drinking and marriage are good activities, not evil ones. Yet Jesus adds that, "*they did not know until the flood came and swept them all away*" (Mt 24:39). So a good life that consists *merely* of eating, drinking, marrying and other good things while being cut off from God is contrary to God's will for our happiness. We were made to know and to love God personally. Yet we cannot know God personally without the grace of Baptism.

As Jesus tells us, *"No one can enter the kingdom of God without being born of water and Spirit"* (John 3:5). Therefore, even people who do many good things still need the grace of Baptism.

What happens, then, to those people who are not Baptised through no fault of their own? Based on Scripture and Tradition, the Church teaches that, while Baptism is necessary for salvation (ccc. 1257), the sanctifying grace of Baptism may sometimes be received without the rite. For example, the Holy Innocents, the children killed by Herod, are recognised as saints, an example of 'Baptism of blood' (Mt 2:16). There is also a 'Baptism of desire' for those who desire Baptism, such as catechumens, and yet die before receiving the sacrament. There may even be many people who are saved because they would desire Baptism explicitly if they knew of its necessity, but who are ignorant through no fault of their own. Yet all these are extraordinary possibilities of grace. Following Christ's explicit command, we should urge people to be converted to Christ and receive Baptism while this sacrament is available to them, for no sacraments can be received after death.

Why Baptise babies when they can't choose and if they have never sinned?

The argument in favour of baptising a child is similar to the argument in favour of conceiving a child. A child did not, after all, choose to be conceived, yet those who mature into adults generally say, in retrospect, that they are glad to be alive. Similarly, Baptism is a second birth that makes the Christian life possible. Those who mature into saints will certainly say, in retrospect, that they are glad that someone baptised them. Furthermore, it is prudent that a child receives Baptism as soon as possible so that this grace can mature.

In the case of a baby, Baptism does not, of course, wash away actual sins for the child has not committed any sins. Yet, like all of us, the child still needs the grace of Baptism, the *second birth*, *"of water and the spirit"* (John 3:5), which frees us from Original Sin and makes us adopted children of God.

Could you explain more about Confirmation? How is it distinct from Baptism?

Confirmation is the sacrament of strengthening and mission, traditionally bestowed on a person who is to going to make a public confession of the Christian faith and face possible opposition. In contrast to Baptism, which is the sacrament of spiritual birth, Confirmation confers spiritual maturity. Hence the one being confirmed is sealed with chrism and the sign of the cross and is strengthened by the gifts of the Holy Spirit, enabling that person to be moved by the Spirit in Christian mission. The clearest Biblical images of the effects of this sacrament are the way in which Jesus is led into the wilderness by the Spirit after his Baptism (Mt 4:1) and how the disciples preach the Gospel to the crowds in Jerusalem after the descent of the Spirit at Pentecost (Acts 2). If we unite our wills freely with the inspiration of the Holy Spirit, we can then be swept up, like the saints, into what is far greater than ourselves. Those goods of this world that have little to do with heaven become pale and insipid, while our love for God and his people is transformed into the fire of divine love.

Further reading. *Compendium* questions 251-270; *Catechism* ccc. 1213-1321 covering especially the sacraments of (i) Baptism (ccc. 1213-1284); (ii) Confirmation (ccc. 1285-1321).

The Eucharistic Miracle of Siena

These hosts, originally consecrated in 1730 and today venerated in the Basilica of St Francis in Siena, have not deteriorated over nearly three centuries. For comparison, unconsecrated hosts kept under similar conditions have been found to decay in less than a decade. While faith in the Eucharist as the Body and Blood of Christ rests principally on the words of Jesus, such Eucharistic miracles also bear witness to this great gift.

The Eucharist

The Eucharist is a sacrifice, a presence and a food. As a *sacrifice* it makes present Jesus Christ's sacrifice on Calvary for our salvation. As a *presence*, it is Jesus Christ himself under the appearances of bread and wine. As a *food*, it is the nourishment of our souls by which we share in God's own life.

Why are there two Eucharistic species, the host and the chalice, instead of just one?

Jesus Christ – body and blood, soul and divinity – is present in the host and the chalice. As a consequence, one receives Communion fully even when one only consumes the host. Nevertheless, God gives us the body and blood of Christ in distinct forms because we participate in the Eucharist as a sacrifice, not only as a sacrament. Since the Eucharist is a sacrifice, the body and blood are separate on the altar just as the blood of Christ was shed from his body on the cross.

Why do Catholics believe that bread and wine become the Body and Blood of Jesus?

We know that Jesus intended the bread and wine to change into his body and blood in the Mass for the following reasons. (1) In John 6, when Jesus promised the 'bread from heaven' which would be his living body, he used the emphases '*real* food' and '*real* drink'. Furthermore, the reaction of his listeners (many of whom abandoned him) shows that they understood 'eat my flesh' (the Greek phrase expresses this notion explicitly) and 'drink my blood' as literal, yet Jesus did not say that they had misunderstood his meaning. (2) Jesus says, *"this is my body"* and *"this is the cup of my blood"*, not *"this represents my body and blood"* (cf. Mt 26:26-28; Mk 14:22-24; Lk 22:17-22; 1 Co 11:23-25). (3) The Passover, which prefigures the Eucharist in the Old Testament, specifies that the flesh of the lamb must be consumed physically. The implication is that Jesus, the Lamb of God of the new Passover, also intends to be consumed by us. (4) St Paul says that *"anyone who eats and drinks without discerning the body eats and drinks judgment upon himself,"* implying the substantial reality of the body of Christ in the Eucharistic meal. (5) Church documents from the first centuries show belief in the substantial presence of the Body and Blood of Christ. St Justin Martyr (c. 152 AD), for example, explicitly denies that the Eucharist is common food and drink, but is, rather, the *"flesh and blood of that Jesus who was made flesh"* (First Apology to the Roman Senate, 66). These sources show that the early Christians understood that Christ had given us his body and blood in a substantial, not a metaphorical sense. (6) Various Eucharistic miracles, such as those of Lanciano, Siena and Bolsena.

The Communion service at my local Anglican or Episcopalian church seems very similar to the Catholic Mass. So why are we not worshipping together?

Those who founded Anglicanism in the sixteenth century wanted to maintain the outward appearance of the kind of liturgy to which people had been accustomed for centuries. Similarly in modern times, an Anglican communion service often follows the general form of the Mass and may even be called a 'Mass'. Nevertheless, Anglican liturgy differs from Catholic liturgy in subtle but important ways. For example, the Catholic priest will say before Communion, *"This is the Lamb of God ..."* whereas the Anglican minister will usually say, *"Jesus is the Lamb of God ..."*. The reason for this change is that Anglicanism, according to its own historical articles of faith, rejects Catholic belief in transubstantiation. Anglican liturgy therefore avoids referring to the host as the Lamb of God. Anglicanism's Thirty-Nine Articles also deny that the Mass is a sacrifice (article 21) and that ordination is a sacrament (article 25). While there are, in fact, some Anglican ministers who believe all of these Catholic teachings, they do so by virtue of their private judgment, not the official teaching of Anglicanism. So we do not celebrate the Eucharist together because an Anglican liturgical service is not a Catholic Mass.

It is also forbidden for non-Catholic Christians to receive Holy Communion at Catholic Mass for two reasons: first, because one must profess complete faith in the Real Presence of Jesus before receiving, and second, because reception of the Eucharist implies full communion with the Church, a unity with all those who gather at the altar of the Lord. As St Paul has said, *"Because there is one, we who are many are one body, for we all partake of the one bread"* (1 Cor 10:17). So communion takes place with unity in faith and not without that unity.

<u>Further reading.</u> *Compendium* questions 271-294; *Catechism* ccc. 1322-1419 especially the: (i) Eucharist in the economy of salvation (ccc. 1333-1344); (ii) sacramental sacrifice: thanksgiving, memorial, presence (ccc. 1356-1381); (iii) paschal banquet (ccc. 1382-1401); (iv) Eucharist as the pledge of glory to come (ccc. 1402-1405).

Pope Benedict XVI hearing Confessions

The Holy Father teaches by word and example about the importance of Confession, a wonderful but somewhat neglected sacrament today. The importance of Confession is also shown by the life of St John Vianney, known as the 'Curé of Ars'. St John Vianney had a gift for reading souls and lifting the heaviest burdens of sin. He regularly preached about Confession and sometimes spent sixteen to eighteen hours a day in the confessional.

Confession and Anointing

Confession (also called *Penance* or *Reconciliation*) is the sacrament by which we, repenting and confessing our sins, are absolved of sin through the ministry of a priest.

Anointing of the Sick is that sacrament by which sick persons, through anointing with oil and the prayer of the priest, receive grace for the salvation of their souls and possible bodily healing.

Why do I need to confess my sins to a priest, if I have already confessed my sins to God?

God wants to forgive us our sins and restore us to the life of grace, but sacramental Confession is God's chosen means for a baptised person to receive forgiveness for serious sin.

The method of verbal confession and absolution from a priest can also be seen as fitting for the following reasons. (1) We relate to God as members of the Church, the Body of Christ, and so God's forgiveness comes to us by means of the Church. (2) We need assurance that we are forgiven, which is what absolution from a priest guarantees. (3) We are notoriously bad at judging ourselves, either being too lax or too harsh; the priest, acting in the person of Christ, brings a steadying objectivity and helps prevent self-deception. (4) When we recognise and acknowledge our sins this helps form a healthy conscience, not an unhealthy and debilitating guilt that may cause despair. (5) Confession is one of the most perfect remedies for pride, the most dangerous of all the sins. By verbally and humbly acknowledging our sins and asking God for forgiveness, we also allow God to cast out our pride and restore our divine love of him and other persons.

Finally, it is not uncommon in modern life for people to make non-sacramental 'confessions' to other public persons or accredited professionals or even through the media. Such secular alternatives cannot restore us to God's grace. Nevertheless, these attempts to seek confessional substitutes for healing and renewed strength do testify, indirectly, to the psychological importance of the sacrament of Confession.

Isn't an indulgence a kind of luxury or some kind of medieval superstition?

In Catholic theology, the word indulgence is neither a kind of luxury nor a medieval superstition. The word indulgence derives from the idea of a kindness or favour, especially by the remission of a tax or a debt. To understand the benefit of this remission, it is important to examine sin and its effects.

Sin separates us from God, but sinful actions also cause all kinds of other damage. To give an analogy, if sin is like a pin we stick in a board and Confession is like taking out the pin, the hole left over is the damage caused by our sin. While absolution removes guilt and re-unites us to God, penance is also necessary to repair this damage. An example of this distinction in Scripture is provided by the story of Zacchaeus, who recognised not only his need for reunion with God, but also the need to repair the damage he had done by defrauding others, "*Behold, Lord, the half of my goods I give to the poor; and if I have defrauded any one of anything, I restore it fourfold*" (Lk 19:8).

Penance is what is done to repair the damage of sin, and a priest will usually set a penance before giving absolution in the context of the sacrament of Confession. Indeed, the existence of a temporary state of Purgatory after death is for the benefit of those persons who die in a state of grace but without completing their penance on earth.

God in his mercy, however, even provides a means of remitting this penance for those who have been reconciled to him. This partial or complete remission, called an indulgence, is granted on the authority of the Church given by Christ (cf. Mt 16:19). These indulgences channel the merits of Christ and the saints to assist sinners to repair the damage of their sins.

Can I be anointed whenever I am ill?

Anointing is meant to be received when a person is seriously ill, injured or frail, in particular when there is foreseeable danger of death. So this sacrament, which is offered at the priest's discretionary judgment, should not be received when a person is well or only mildly ill. On the other hand, it is not necessary to wait until someone is at the point of death before he or she receives Anointing (ccc. 1514). It is fitting, for example, that a person receives the sacrament just prior to a serious operation. Furthermore, if the person regains health and deteriorates subsequently, the sacrament may be repeated.

Further reading. *Compendium* questions 295-320; *Catechism* ccc. 1420-1532, covering especially: (i) the importance of Confession (ccc. 1425-1429); (ii) the conversion of the baptised (ccc. 1427-1429); (iii) the sacrament of Penance and Reconciliation (ccc. 1440-1449); (iv) the Anointing of the Sick (ccc. 1499-1532).

Blessed Zélie and Louis Martin
parents of St Thérèse of Lisieux, Doctor of the Church

The good fruits of a holy marriage, or the life of a holy priest or religious, are beyond human measure. The fruitfulness of the marriage of Blessed Zélie and Louis Martin is shown by the life of their daughter, St Thérèse, who entered religious life *"to save souls, and especially to pray for priests."* Since her death at the age of 24, St Thérèse has touched the lives of millions of people. Her relics attracted a quarter of a million pilgrims during a tour of England in 2009.

Marriage and Holy Orders

Marriage is that sacrament by which a baptised man and woman are bound together by vows to an exclusive lifelong commitment to one another and to accepting and raising children. In this sacrament God gives grace for the fulfilment of these duties.

Holy Orders is the sacrament in which a baptised man receives the authority and ability to share in the particular mission that Christ entrusted to his apostles. There are three orders of this sacrament: episcopate, presbyterate and diaconate.

Why is marriage important, especially when many people today have sexual relationships and conceive children outside of marriage?

Practically all human cultures have recognised the importance of marriage of some kind, at least to assist in establishing stability for raising children. Societies that descend into sexual anarchy do not tend to be good environments for raising children in the longer term. The importance of marriage can also be seen by what has accompanied its decline in recent years, such as the increase in unwanted pregnancies, sexually transmitted disease and loneliness. Co-habitation is not an adequate alternative to marriage since it lacks any basis except mutual, provisional agreement. Furthermore, co-habiting couples who subsequently marry are more likely to divorce than those who do not co-habit prior to their marriage. Finally, the greatness and glory of sacramental marriage is seen in its fruitfulness, especially in the lives of holy couples such as Blessed Zélie and Louis Martin (*see page 62*).

What is the justification for the existence of a sacrament of Holy Orders?

Justification for the existence of Holy Orders and a Christian priesthood can be seen in Jesus' commissioning of twelve apostles and the bestowing on them of unique authority, such as the forgiveness of sins (Jn 20:23). The need for an ordained Christian priesthood, described in Scripture as the 'order of Melchizedek' (cf. Heb 5:1, 7:17), is also implied by the nature of the Eucharist as a sacrifice. The commissioning of deacons by ordination is also attested in Scripture (cf. Acts 6:6) Furthermore, the apostles ordained others to succeed them. St Paul, for example, ordained St Timothy (2 Tim 1:6). This principle of apostolic succession is also recognised explicitly by St Clement, the third bishop of Rome after St Peter, in a letter towards the end of the first century, "*They (the apostles) appointed those (ministers) already mentioned, and afterwards gave instructions, that when these should fall asleep, other approved men should succeed them in their ministry*" (Corinthians, 44). So the threefold sacrament of Holy Orders is rooted in Scripture and the principle of apostolic succession was recognised by Christians from the first century.

Why can't we have women priests and married priests?

Priesthood is a kind of spiritual fatherhood, as St Paul implies when writing to the Corinthians, addressing them as his children, "*I became your father in Christ Jesus through the gospel*" (1 Cor 4:15). Hence priesthood is, by its nature, male, just as motherhood is, by its nature, female. Furthermore, those with Holy Orders act in the person of Jesus Christ, who was incarnate as a man, and who chose only men as his apostles, even though his close disciples included men and women. While some ecclesial groups have women ministers, such associations do not formally recognise priesthood to be a sacrament or the Mass to be a sacrifice.

While only men are ordained, however, Catholicism has proved unusual in having many prominent women in its history and among its greatest teachers. The Church has canonised many women saints and St Teresa of Avila, St Catherine of Siena and St Thérèse of Lisieux are recognised as doctors of the Church. Furthermore, Catholicism has given a singular honour to a woman, Mary, the Mother of God. One consequence is that Catholicism has both a strong feminine and a strong masculine aspect to its culture and history.

With a few exceptions, the Church does not ordain married men. One reason is simply that marriage and Holy Orders involve a call to a service of love that is all-consuming (cf. 1 Cor 7:32-33). To be fruitful, the commitment to each vocation must be complete and it is difficult for a man to do both.

Further reading. *Compendium* questions 321-350; *Catechism* ccc. 1533-1666, covering: (i) the sacrament of Holy orders in the economy of salvation (ccc. 1539-1553); (ii) the three degrees of the sacrament of Holy Orders (ccc. 1554-1571); (iii) the effects of the sacrament of Holy Orders (ccc. 1581-1589); (iv) Marriage in God's Plan (ccc. 1602-1620); (v) matrimonial consent (ccc. 1625-1637); (vi) the effects of Matrimony (ccc. 1638-1642); (vii) the goods and requirements of conjugal love (ccc. 1643-1654).

The Temptation of Christ by Duccio di Buoninsegna

Christ was victorious over the devil's temptations in the wilderness.
If we call upon his help we can share in his victory over sin.

Moral Action

A moral action is any action that proceeds from our deliberate will. We have responsibility for such actions, all of which are either good or evil. A sin is a deliberate evil action: a thought, word, deed or omission contrary to God's will.

If God can do anything, why can't he simply make us good?

The power of God does not extend to contradiction. God created human beings with free will, intending us to be his adopted children in glory, not his puppets. If he were to override our freedom, forcing us to be good, he would contradict his gift and his love and we would cease to be the kinds of beings he created. So while God desires us to be saved, he respects our choices, even if we choose to reject him.

Hasn't science proven that human freedom and moral choice is an illusion, that all human actions are determined by the motions of our atoms or by our genes?

The idea that the behaviour of atoms has proved that we lack free will is based on the idea that the atoms of our bodies move like little billiard balls. Since billiard balls do not choose what to do, but follow laws of motion, anything made up of atoms, such as ourselves, must – it is argued – also lack the ability to choose. The problem with this argument, however, is that we are not the mere sum of our parts. Even if atoms were like little billiard balls, which they are not, the atoms of our bodies are bound into ourselves. We therefore move our atoms rather than being moved by them. So we cannot use the fact that free atoms do not choose where to go to prove that we do not choose our actions. With regard to genes, it is true that our genes influence our behaviour, but so do many other things, such as our friendships and the state of the weather. To influence us, however, is not the same as determining us, as if we do not also choose our actions. In addition, if our genes were to make our moral choices for us, all genetically identical twins would make the same moral choices, a prediction that is not, in fact, observed in reality.

Why should just one mortal sin kill the divine life of the soul?

The idea of one mortal sin depriving a human soul of grace seems harsh if one thinks of God as sentencing potential saints to damnation for a single infraction of his law, like one traffic offence in an otherwise blameless journey. The Christian relationship to God does not consist, however, in achieving a perfect track record to gain admission to heaven, but loving God with one's whole being, a relationship that will be consummated in heaven. Scripture even describes this relationship by the intimate image of a marriage covenant (Eph 5:31-32). Consequently, to commit a mortal sin is not like failing to make the grade in a test of one's perfection, but is more like an act of adultery in which one surrenders to something else (the world, the flesh or the devil) other than God (cf. Ez 16:32). Therefore, just as a single act of adultery requires subsequent reconciliation with one's spouse for the relationship to be restored, so too a single mortal sin requires reconciliation, ordinarily by the sacrament of Confession, for the one's relationship with God to be restored.

You claim that God gives us victory over sin, but why is it that I am so often defeated?

First, it is important to be patient. God cultivates saints and total victory over sin can take a long time, even an entire lifetime. Second, it is important to remember that we cannot perfect ourselves; indeed, self-perfection is an ancient heresy called Pelagianism. The path to victory over sin is not, therefore, a matter of becoming strong-willed by ourselves, but of deepening our union with God, by means of the sacraments and prayer, so that the love of God grows in us and the attractions of sin weaken. Our main task as Christians, therefore, is to remain in Christ, like a branch attached to a vine, so that his divine life can flow into us and purify us. Finally, we should be comforted by the fact that even a defeat can be turned into a victory by God's grace. When Peter denied knowing Jesus out of fear, Scripture tells us that Peter *"went out and wept bitterly"* (Mt 26:75). Yet an outcome of this defeat was that Peter's pride was broken at the deepest level. Relying on God's grace rather than his own strength, Peter was then ready to act as leader of the Church.

Further reading. *Compendium* questions 363-376 and 391-400; *Catechism* covering especially (i) the spiritual battle (ccc. 407-409); (ii) concupiscence (ccc. 1264); (iii) human freedom (ccc. 1730-1748); (iv) the morality of human acts (ccc. 1749-1761); (v) conscience (ccc. 1776-1802); (vi) sin (ccc. 1846-1876).

C. S. Lewis (1898-1963)

Lewis was a devout Christian, an Oxford don and a friend of J. R. R. Tolkien. While Lewis is probably most well known today for his children's books, *The Chronicles of Narnia*, he wrote a defence of natural law in *The Abolition of Man*.

Natural Law and the Ten Commandments

MORALS

> The natural law, known by reason, is the universal moral law of human nature for living well.
>
> The Ten Commandments are the ten universal laws given directly by God to Moses on Mount Sinai.

Didn't Jesus preach a gospel of love, not laws and commandments?

This question is based on a false assumption, that laws and love are incompatible. Those things that are mandated by just moral laws, especially the Ten Commandments, are practical expressions of God's love for us, since they articulate what is compatible with our happiness. Furthermore, those who grow in the friendship of God have a stronger desire to keep God's commandments, even when their observance involves some sacrifice, since they have come to love with God what God loves, as St Thomas Aquinas observes (ST 2a2ae, q.29, a.3).

Is getting to heaven simply a matter of keeping the commandments?

To claim that getting to heaven is simply a matter of keeping the commandments, is like saying that the secret of a successful marriage is not to commit adultery. Clearly, unrepented adultery is incompatible with a good marriage, yet one could carefully avoid adultery throughout one's whole life while having no love for one's spouse whatsoever. In a similar way, breaking God's commandments is incompatible with loving God. Yet it does not follow that anyone who keeps God's commandments actually loves God. One might, for example, be motivated to be moral by the desire to earn salvation from God in the manner of a business transaction, or even be motivated out of pride in one's own perfection. Given, however, that heaven is the eternal dwelling place of those who love God, a person who keeps the commandments but is lacking in divine love cannot enter heaven.

Didn't some of Jesus' disciples sometimes infringe the moral law?

Moral precepts can be divided into two groups. One kind of precept is an absolute law, the law being 'absolute' insofar as any action that breaks this law is intrinsically evil, regardless of circumstances. So, for example, "*You shall not commit adultery*," (Ex 20:14) is absolute, so that a person who commits adultery commits a sin. Other moral precepts, however, are dependent on circumstances. So the precept, "*Wash your hands before eating*," promotes health and respect, but if, due to circumstances, one is unable to wash one's hands before eating, one is blameless of sin. One of the strategies of evil, however, is to confuse us about these two groups of precepts: the absolute moral laws are reduced to the level of suggestions or ideals, whereas the circumstantial precepts are elevated to the status of absolute laws, making the moral law into a tyrant. So when Jesus' disciples are accused of not washing their hands before eating, Jesus observes how their accusers have found excuses to avoid giving honour to parents (Mt 15:1-20; Mk 7:1-23). In other words, those complaining about the apostles keeping precepts that were not absolute have themselves broken absolute precepts.

Are the commandments consistent? In particular, the commandment, 'You shall not kill,' seems to contradict the apparent legitimacy of a just war.

Any killing that is done as a private act of murder is absolutely forbidden by the fifth commandment. Lawful authority can, however, direct a society to engage in warfare to prevent great evils, such as the destruction or enslavement of that society. Even so, many conditions, such as a legitimate cause and good intention, must be met for such actions to be justified, and ways to avoid killing should be chosen if possible (ccc. 2302-2317).

Are Christians hypocrites insofar as they do not keep God's commandments?

Only one person, besides Christ, has ever lived entirely free of all sin, but this failure does not mean that all Christians are hypocrites. Christians, rather, acknowledge their need for forgiveness and God's grace. In other words, rather than being an assembly of the perfect, the Church on earth is more like a hospital for sinners who want to become saints.

Further reading. *Compendium* questions 415-421 and 434-533; *Catechism*: ccc. 1949-1964 and ccc. 2052-2557, covering especially: (i) the natural law (ccc. 1954-1960); (ii) the Decalogue (ccc. 2056-2082); (iii) the individual commandments (ccc. 2083-2557).

Mother Teresa of Calcutta (1910-1997)

Grace can be discerned most clearly by its fruitfulness in the lives of holy people and most especially in the lives of the saints. Although the effects of grace vary, some common characteristics include the tendency to relate to other persons as one's brothers and sisters in Christ, to pray for one's enemies and to regard worldly matters from the perspective of eternal life.

Grace and the Beatitudes MORALS

What is Grace?

Grace refers to those gifts that bring about a supernatural friendship with God. 'Supernatural' means an elevation of human nature beyond what it is naturally capable of attaining.

The Beatitudes are eight states of blessedness proclaimed by Christ in the Sermon on the Mount (Mt 5:3-11). These states manifest the life of heaven on earth, bringing a foretaste and promise of joy even amid earthly suffering.

Since grace is invisible, how do we know grace is real?

Grace is a quality of the soul and, like all qualities of the soul, grace is not directly visible to us. Such qualities can, however, be known from their effects on the way a person lives. Now the effects of grace are very diverse, shown by the remarkable variety of the saints. Nevertheless, there are certain general characteristics of a mature life of grace. First, one's stance towards other human beings changes, since, as an adopted child of God, all other living human beings become one's actual or potential brothers and sisters. Second, one's stance towards the world changes. Many things that are often seen as important, such as material possessions, become trivial in themselves. Conversely, many things that seem trivial to other people, such as small actions done with great love, take on eternal significance. Therefore, although mature Christians rarely withdraw from the world in a physical way, they are different, and are often perceived as different by their contemporaries, *"Their days are passed on the earth, though their citizenship is above in the heavens"* (Epistle to Diognetus, 5). So although grace is not visible directly, the effects of grace can be perceived in the lives of those who show its fruits.

In what way is human nature lacking that we also need grace?

Human nature has the ability to discover that there is a God, but it is only by grace that we can know God personally as his adopted children. Hence one of the prayers of Christianity is the *Our Father*, which is not addressed to a distant God, but to a loving Father by those born into the life of grace.

There are various standard mistakes about the relationship between nature and grace. *Pelagianism* implies that nature alone is sufficient for us to achieve Christian perfection. *Determinism* is a distorted view of grace, implying grace entirely overrides nature, so that human choices have no bearing on salvation. *Modernism* takes many forms, but essentially dissolves the distinction between nature and grace entirely.

If Christians have grace, why do so many Christians seem much like everyone else?

Many persons who have received Baptism and become Christians subsequently lose grace through mortal sin. Until the restoration of grace, usually through the sacrament of Confession, such persons are like dead branches and cannot bear the fruits of grace. Many other Christians live a kind of dual life. They remain occupied, at least in part, by the search for happiness in this passing world. Jesus described this condition as being like seed thrown among thorns, where the seed is the Word of God and the thorns are the cares of the world and the delight in riches. These thorns choke the life of grace, and it proves unfruitful (Mt 13:22).

Nevertheless, the relatively few Christians who surrender to God's grace with a full heart can quite rapidly show the fruits of this grace in radically transformed lives. These fruits can be seen most clearly in the lives of the great saints, such as St Francis of Assisi and St Catherine of Siena.

Don't the states that are called 'blessed' in the Beatitudes – especially poverty, mourning, meekness, hunger, thirst and persecution – seem to be a curse rather than a blessing?

Some of the conditions praised in the Beatitudes might seem like a curse taken in isolation, but they can be a blessing in the context of knowing God, in comparison to which other goods become pale and empty. St Paul, for instance, says that he has suffered the loss of 'all things'. Yet he adds that he counts such things as worthless refuse in comparison to the surpassing worth of knowing Christ Jesus the Lord (cf. Phil 3:8).

Further reading. *Compendium* questions 358-362; 384-390 and 422-428; *Catechism*: (i) the Beatitudes (ccc. 1716-1729); (ii) the theological virtues and gifts of the Holy Spirit (ccc. 1812-1845); (iii) the natural law (ccc. 1965-1687); (iv) justification (ccc. 1987-1995); (v) grace (ccc. 1996-2004); (vi) merit (ccc. 2006-2011).

The Seven Deadly Sins by Hieronymous Bosch

Clockwise from the bottom:
anger, envy, avarice, gluttony, sloth, lust and pride.

Jesus Christ is shown in the centre,
symbolising his grace to help us overcome these vices.

Virtues and Vices

MORALS

Virtues are good habits, that is, they give us a disposition to perform good actions. Vices are evil habits; that is, they give us a disposition to perform evil actions.

Why is it that people with God's grace remain afflicted with vices?

The vices that a person has acquired, through repeated evil actions, are rarely eliminated immediately when that person surrenders to God's grace. Nevertheless, although a vice is a dangerous evil, to have a vice is not, in itself, to be in a state of sin. A person only falls into sin when he or she surrenders to the vice rather than to God. Furthermore, when vices are not indulged, and the soul is filled with the love of God, such vices are powerless and will, in practice, gradually fade away.

Why does the word 'virtuous' imply, in some social contexts, that a person is boring?

In certain situations, such as war, many virtues like courage are self-evidently good and praiseworthy. In times of apparent peace, however, and especially in self-indulgent and narcissistic societies, at least some vices are praised and the word 'virtuous' can almost become derogatory, implying that a person is dull or boring. The reality, however, is that someone who is virtuous in the Christian sense, that is, on fire with the love of God, is like someone standing in a great light, illuminating the whole world and giving colour to everything. By contrast, those afflicted with vices and committing associated sins are drowning in darkness: their whole world becomes dull, dreary and empty. Whatever else can be said about the great saints and the sufferings they endure, their recorded lives on earth can scarcely be described as dull and uninteresting. Indeed, the lives of the saints are often characterised by an extraordinary range of experiences and achievements, even by the standards of the world. By contrast, it is striking how many lives of the great sinners (think, for example, of celebrities today who lead very immoral lives) end in suicide, loneliness or premature death.

I am confused by the word 'pride'. Is it always wrong, for example, to 'take pride' in one's own achievements and should a Christian deliberately avoid greatness?

Christians are called to greatness of all kinds, as can be seen, for example, in the lives of the saints and the beauty of the Church's art. St Thomas Aquinas, the greatest teacher of Christian virtue ethics, even describes the disposition to strive for greatness, in the context of union with God, as a special virtue. This virtue, called *magnanimity*, is like a crown of all the virtues. Now the vice of pride and the virtue of magnanimity might seem similar, in that both imply the desire for greatness. Magnanimous persons, however, desire greatness in loving union with God and acknowledge their dependence on God. Proud persons, by contrast, try to make themselves great or to measure their success by the failures of others – as in the parable of the Pharisee and the tax collector (Lk 18:10-14). What makes magnanimity different from pride can also be seen in the New Testament song of Mary, the *Magnificat*. Mary affirms her own greatness when she says, "*Henceforth all generations will call me blessed*" (Lk 1:48). She adds, however, that her greatness comes entirely as a gift from God, "*For he who is mighty has done great things for me*" (Lk 1:49) and rejoices that many others will benefit (Lk 1:54). The *Magnificat* therefore shows how one can aspire to greatness in union with God and even rejoice in one's own greatness without being proud.

What is the difference between love and lust? Can sexual desire ever be good?

God made us male and female with the desire for sexual union, the fruit of which is the gift of new life, a person with an immortal soul. When this sexual union is in the context of the sacrament of marriage, blessed by God, then sexual union can be a great good as well as God's chosen way to bring children into existence, possible future saints in the kingdom of heaven. Consequently, the sexual desire that accompanies this action is an authentic form of love, since the strong desire for sexual union is in harmony with a desire for the good of one's husband or wife, the good that God desires and the good of the child, if a child is conceived. When, however, the desire for pleasure is present without a desire for these other goods, then sexual desire is disordered, often reducing the other person to the status of a de-personalised object. Under these circumstances, sexual desire is evil and is called lust.

Further reading. *Compendium* questions 377-383; *Catechism*: ccc. 1803-1844, covering especially (i) the cardinal virtues (ccc. 1805-1809); (ii) the theological virtues (ccc. 1812-1829).

Pope John Paul II

Pope John Paul II, who served as Supreme Pontiff of the Catholic Church from 1978 to 2005, travelled to over one hundred countries bearing the message of Christian hope for the world. Among the fruits of his ministry, he is credited with being instrumental in the fall of communism in Eastern Europe, both through his teaching and his three pastoral visits to Communist Poland, which brought millions of his countrymen onto the streets.

Christian Life in the World

MORALS

> The personal Christian life is the confirming of one's life to the pattern of Jesus Christ.
>
> The public Christian life is the conforming of one's own family and society to the pattern of Jesus Christ.

Human needs seem to be without end. How, then, can one ever complete all the corporal and spiritual works of mercy that are needed?

We are not required to meet every human need by ourselves and God regards the love with which we give more highly than the amount that we give (Mk 12:41-44). Furthermore, the Church is a spiritual body in which persons have distinct roles. We should not be anxious, therefore, that we cannot perform every kind of service, but we should aim to fulfill the tasks of our own vocation in fidelity and love (cf. 1 Cor 12:27-31). Nevertheless, we must not reject those around us who need our help, when we can and should give help (cf. Mt 25:31-46).

We are often told about the importance of evangelisation, but where does one begin?

Fruitful evangelisation is based on the twofold principle of spirit and truth. With regard to truth, Christianity is a revealed faith, so it is necessary to receive its truth in order to communicate this truth to others. Therefore, it is important to invest time, insofar as one is able, into learning about the faith from reliable teachers, especially the saints and doctors of the Church. Truth alone, however, is not enough. One must also be moved by the Holy Spirit in order to be fruitful. So one must come to know God personally, especially through devotion to daily prayer and the sacraments, to be moved by God effectively to this work of proclaiming the Gospel. So true evangelisation begins, in fact, with study and prayer, so that this work, as God's work, will be fruitful.

I struggle to understand and follow the Church's teaching on sex. What do you suggest?

The struggle to be chaste is not an exclusively modern challenge, as sexual desires are powerful, especially in the young. What is new in modern times, however, is that many societies have ceased, for the most part, to promote the principle that sexual acts are for marriage and procreation. On the contrary, promiscuity is often encouraged, together with the widespread promotion of contraceptives to prevent pregnancies, and abortion to dispose of the many unwanted children who are, nevertheless, still conceived. This massive reversal of public values and policies has left the Catholic Church almost alone in defending the original purpose of sex, namely the procreation of children in the context of the union of husband and wife. When the struggle to be chaste has been made far more difficult because of these social pressures, how, then, can one follow the Church's teaching in this area?

To answer this question, it is important to think, first, about why chastity is important and then how one might live more chastely. To be chaste is not to be against sex, but to have some awareness of what sex really means. The natural outcome of the sexual act is a child, a being whose soul will live forever, and who may become a saint, an adopted child of God in the glory of heaven. So, of its nature, sexual union is not a trivial or casual action. Consequently, God has provided the sacrament of marriage to give the proper context and graces for this union to be chaste, joyful and fruitful. It should also be noted that relationships that follow God's law are not only fruitful in terms of their offspring, but also in the love of the husband and wife. One sign of this fruitfulness is that couples who practise natural family planning (NFP) rather than using contraception have very low divorce rates.

Nevertheless, chastity is difficult today even for those who understand these principles and strive to be chaste. What, then, can help promote victory? A wholesome personal environment is a great help, such as good friendships and outgoing activities. It is also important to avoid bad company and influences, especially those many aspects of the media that promote lust. As a spiritual battle, it is also essential to rely on spiritual resources: when one's life is filled with the love of God and the things of God, such as the works of mercy, there is no room for lust. Finally, many people do not experience immediate victory in this area, yet God will give final victory to those who repent of sin and seek his help.

Further reading. *Compendium* questions 401-414 and 428-433; *Catechism* covering especially: (i) the human person and society (ccc. 1877-1948); (ii) Christian holiness (ccc. 2012-2016); (iii) the precepts of the Church (ccc. 2041-2043); (iv) the family and society (ccc. 2201-2246); (v) life issues (ccc. 2270-2283); (vi) Marriage and chastity (ccc. 2351-2400).

The Meditative Prayer of St Dominic by Fra Angelico

The life of St Dominic, like all the saints whose lives are recorded, bears witness to the importance and fruitfulness of personal prayer.

The Life of Prayer

> Prayer is speaking and listening to God and desiring to be united with God and to do his will.

How do I know that God hears my prayers?

The all-powerful God who created the universe out of love hears not only our spoken prayers, but even the prayers 'spoken' in our minds. Furthermore, Psalm 94(93) explicitly affirms that the Lord sees and hears everything that happens and even knows our thoughts. Jesus Christ affirms the same teaching, telling us that our heavenly Father sees all that is done in secret, "*Go to your private room, shut yourself in, and so pray to your Father who is in that secret place, and your Father who sees all that is done in secret will reward you*" (Matthew 6:6 NJB). In this text, Jesus therefore confirms that God hears our prayers and will reward our prayers, even if we are not aware of his presence. So we know that God hears our prayers, both from the fact that he is God and all-powerful, and from explicit revelations in Scripture, including the words of Christ himself.

How do I know that it is the true God that I am communicating with in prayer?

This is an important question as there is a real possibility of deception in the life of prayer. How do I know, for example, that I am not simply listening to some projection of my own imagination – or even some other spiritual being who may be malign rather than good? Such difficulties are compounded by the fact that a good deal of contemporary 'spirituality' is not even Christian at all. Such 'spirituality' often encourages a person to focus on created things in the absence of Christian revelation, or to meditate simply on oneself and one's feelings, lacking the Holy Trinity as its focus.

So an important way to authenticate what one hears, or the prompts that one is given, is to test them against revelation. Scripture, Tradition and the Magisterium of the Church express the Catholic faith, and any apparent spiritual insights that clearly contradict what has been revealed cannot be authentic. Simple common sense is also important. One ought to have a healthy scepticism, for example, if a purported prophet claims to have heard God giving him permission to acquire great wealth for his own use, to rape prisoners of war, to steal or to lie. The Father of Our Lord Jesus Christ is a God of love, as shown in the life of Christ, not a god of hatred, lust or any of the seven deadly sins. Furthermore, as one grows in the Christian life, one acquires a sense for what is genuine. As Jesus says, *"My sheep hear my voice, and I know them, and they follow me ... A stranger they will not follow, but they will flee from him, for they do not know the voice of strangers"* (John 10:27,5). So one tends to become more astute in following the voice of the true God to whom one is praying.

In addition, a great help to praying authentically is to use the words that God has revealed in Scripture and Tradition or through the lives of the saints, such as the Psalms, the Lord's Prayer, the Hail Mary, the prayers of the Church's liturgy and a great variety of Catholic devotions. Such prayers raise our minds and hearts beyond our natural aspirations and have proved their fruitfulness repeatedly in the lives of the saints.

Finally, another important sign of authentic communication with God is that the true God will sometimes ask us to do things that are difficult, involving personal sacrifice. When Moses first encountered God on Mount Horeb, he did not want to return to Egypt to free the people of Israel as God asked him (Ex 3:1 – 4:17). In a similar way today, God may sometimes reveal to us in prayer that we need to do certain things that we find difficult. In such situations, we are at least unlikely to be listening to a projection of our own desires.

What is wrong with simply treating my work as my prayer, if I am living a good life?

While living a good life is one way in which we give glory to God, it is important to clear about what a 'good life' really means. From the perspective of God, no human life is entirely good that has no place for God, because God made us to know him and love him. When one is working, however, one's principal focus is on one's working activity, not on God. So we cannot simply treat our work as our prayer. Furthermore, time set aside for prayer does not detract from our productivity at other times. God says, "*I am like an evergreen cypress, from me comes your fruit*" (Hosea 14:8). In other words, our fruitfulness comes from God and, if we pray to God, our lives and work will also be fruitful.

Further reading. *Compendium* questions 534-556, 567-577; *Catechism*: (i) the nature of prayer (ccc. 2559-2565); (ii) prayer in the Bible (ccc. 2566-2622); (iii) prayer in the Church and its Tradition (ccc. 2623-2662); (iv) ways of praying (ccc. 2663-2696); (v) the life of prayer (ccc. 2697-2724); (vi) the battle of prayer (ccc. 2725-2758).

The Agony in the Garden by Giovanni Bellini

Jesus not only taught his disciples the words of the Lord's Prayer, but often himself prayed to his heavenly Father. The words he spoke during his agony before his Passion are a variation on the third petition of the Lord's Prayer, "*Not my will, but thine, be done*" (Lk 22:42).

The Lord's Prayer

The 'Lord's Prayer', also called the *Our Father*, is the prayer Jesus taught his disciples when they asked him to teach them to pray.

Why should the Lord's Prayer be so important when the words seem so simple?

The most direct response to the question of the importance of the Lord's Prayer is that this prayer is from Jesus Christ himself, when he answered his disciples' request to teach them to pray. So for the simple reason that the Son of God has taught us this prayer, we can be assured that this is a perfect prayer – pleasing to God and beneficial to ourselves.

Furthermore, although the words of the Lord's Prayer are so straightforward that they can be taught to young children, these words are profound, referring to realities that exceed the natural reach of the human mind. St Thomas Aquinas also identifies five exemplary qualities of the Lord's Prayer: this prayer is *confident*, addressing the Father in calm expectation; this prayer is *well ordered*, starting with God, heavenly things and then earthly things; this prayer is *suitable*, insofar as we ask only for what is good for us; this prayer is *devout*, insofar as it flows from a love of God and neighbour; and finally it is *humble*, insofar as we recognise our need of God's help, without demanding or trying to buy God's help.

Is it a worthless action to pray the Lord's Prayer many times, using the same words?

To repeat the words of the Lord's Prayer and other prayers (as we do, for example, when praying the Rosary) can be highly beneficial for us, provided such prayer does not degenerate into empty repetition. After all, once we know the words of the Lord's Prayer and other prayers, we can focus on God, using God's own words, without worrying about finding the right way to express ourselves. Furthermore, it is not necessarily cold and impersonal to say the same thing to someone repeatedly. If, for example, a husband says to his wife, "*I love you*," for the third time in a day, she will not, one might hope, be offended. At least she is unlikely to say, "*Stop all that vain repetition! I have that information already!*" Similarly in the case of our relationship with God, our purpose in praying is not to provide God with information. Indeed, as Jesus says, "*Your Father knows what you need before you ask him*" (Matt 6:8). Our prayers instead help nurture our relationship with God, from which many blessings flow for ourselves and others. Therefore, just as some things are worth repeating in human relationships, so also in our personal relationship with God. Nevertheless, when we repeat very familiar prayers, we should always try to keep in mind that it is a personal God whom we are addressing, not mouthing words to fulfil a quota.

If Jesus taught us this one prayer, why do we have so many other set prayers today?

The Lord's Prayer is not the only prayer revealed by God. There is a vast wealth of prayers in Scripture and Tradition, one example being the 150 Psalms of the Old Testament.

Another example is the Hail Mary, part of which comes from the Gospel of Luke (Lk 1:28.42) and part from the writings of the early Church. Many of these revealed prayers are incorporated into the liturgical life of the Church and at least some of them ought to be part of our personal daily prayer life. Furthermore, just as the Lord's Prayer should be committed to memory, it is a good investment to spend time committing a rich variety of other revealed, holy prayers to memory. Such memorisation is like constructing a 'cathedral of the mind' as a dwelling place for the Holy Spirit.

Shouldn't we try to pray without words, as in transcendental meditation?

While many Christians today think that achieving the highest forms of prayer involves emptying the mind in wordless meditation, it is important to remember that Jesus teaches us to pray using words. While the saints sometimes speak of contemplative prayer as a vision that outruns language, this gift does not refute the importance of words. In fact in Scripture, prayer is almost always associated with spoken words, and one of the titles of Jesus himself is the *Logos*, or 'Word'. So we should not be afraid of using words to pray or to think that words are only for beginners in the spiritual life. We should draw especially from Scripture and Tradition for our words in prayer, since these words are inspired by God.

Further reading. *Compendium* questions 578-598; *Catechism*: (i) ccc. 2759-2865, especially: (i) an introduction to the Lord's Prayer (ccc. 2759-2776); (ii) summary statements about the Lord's Prayer (ccc. 2797-2802); (iii) concluding remarks (ccc. 2857-2865).

Pope Benedict XVI distributing Holy Communion

The Holy Father gives a great example of love, reverence and dignity when he offers the Sacrifice of the Mass.

Praying the Mass

PRAYER

Praying the Mass is the fully conscious and active participation in the Eucharist. This is the prayerful engagement in the Mass, aided by proper understanding, good preparation and the application of its power and blessings to our lives.

Where can I find the texts of the prayers of the Mass?

The Mass prayers can be found in books called 'Missals', which are available from Catholic publishers such as the CTS. As a Missal may seem complex at first, however, it is worth asking someone for a lesson in navigating through these books. It is also important to be aware that there is some variety in the approved rites and forms of the Mass.

The Mass doesn't seem to be in the Bible, so where did the Mass come from?

All the principal elements of the Mass are, in fact, in the Bible, drawn together into a liturgical form by the early Christians under the guidance of the Holy Spirit. Indeed, the central action, the transubstantiation of the bread and wine into the body and blood of Jesus Christ is taken directly from the accounts of Jesus' words at the Last Supper when he instituted the Eucharist, "*This is my body ... this is the cup of my Blood, the blood of the new and everlasting covenant ... Do this in memory of me*" (I Cor 11:23-25; Mt 26:26-28; Mk 14:22-24; Lk 22:17-20).

Other Biblical sources for the Mass include its two main divisions, the Liturgy of the Word and the Liturgy of the Eucharist, which are prefigured in the liturgy of the Synagogue (cf. Lk 4:16-39) and the liturgy of the Temple sacrifices (cf. Ezra 6:19-22). Among the many other elements of the Mass drawn from the Bible, the opening words, *"The grace of the Lord Jesus Christ and the love of God and the fellowship of the Holy Spirit be with you all,"* conclude St Paul's second letter to the Corinthians, and the words *"Lord, I am not worthy to receive you ..."* are the words of the centurion to Jesus (Mt 8:8). Many ritual aspects of the Mass, such as incense and vestments, are prefigured in the Old Testament (cf. Lev 8) as *"a shadow of the good things to come,"* (Heb 10:1). The 'good thing' that has come is the perfect sacrifice of the Mass, which makes Christ's sacrifice present to all ages until the end of time.

Important evidence for the existence of the Mass in the early Church is also affirmed by early Christian writings. For example, St Justin Martyr's *First Apology to the Roman Senate*, written about the middle of the second century, provides a detailed account of the Eucharistic liturgy. St Justin describes many elements – including readings, a sermon, the kiss of peace, the offertory, a Eucharistic prayer of thanksgiving, the consecration by the words of institution, intercessions, the great 'Amen' and the communion – all of which are familiar parts of the Mass today. St Justin also describes the Eucharist in Catholic terms as the *"flesh and blood of that Jesus who was made flesh"* (*First Apology*, 66), and St Irenaeus, also in the second century, claims that the Church offers the 'pure sacrifice' (*Against Heresies*, IV, 18). Therefore, while there has clearly been some elaboration of the details of the Mass over the centuries, the Mass is sourced from Scripture, was developed into a liturgical form in the early Church, and has a structure today that has a consistent, organic coherence with its origins.

Why can't a divorced and re-married person receive Communion?

In fact, no one in a state of grave sin should receive Communion, based on St Paul's words, "*Whoever, therefore, eats the bread or drinks the cup of the Lord in an unworthy manner will be guilty of profaning the body and blood of the Lord*" (1 Cor 11:27). Marriage vows are made 'until death do us part'. So a marital relationship in which one of the spouses is already bound to another person by a valid marriage entails breaking a solemn vow made before God, unless the original marriage has been judged by the Church to be null and void because of some impediment (an annulment). As Jesus warns (Mk 10:11-12), such a relationship is adultery, which is a grave sin, so long as both spouses who made the original vow remain alive. So a person in such a condition of life should not receive Communion.

At the same time, it is important to recognise that many people come to faith later in life, with complex personal backgrounds and not fully realising the significance of their commitments earlier in life. If someone desires Communion and yet, in obedience, respectfully refrains from Communion because of being in an irregular relationship, this is another way in which to honour and bear witness to the Eucharist. Furthermore, God is capable of all things, and by his grace even the most complex personal situations can be resolved.

Further reading. *Compendium* questions 271-294 (on the sacrament); *Catechism* ccc. 1345-1355 (liturgical celebration of the Eucharist).

The Return of the Prodigal Son by Rembrandt

The parable of the Prodigal Son (Lk 15:11-32), welcomed home by his loving Father, is a Biblical image of what takes place in Confession.

The Practice of Confession

> The practice of Confession is the means by which we receive absolution of our sins; the sacrament also helps us to avoid sin and grow in virtue.

Do I need to confess all my sins? Is it enough to just confess a tendency to sin?

When examining such questions regarding Confession, the example of a personal relationship such as a marriage may help shed light on the issues. In any personal relationship, it is clear that an act of reconciliation requires us to acknowledge the specific hurts that we have caused the other person. It is not enough to express general regret for a tendency to hurt the other, or sorrow for just one of many causes of grief. If, for example, a husband hurts his wife both by committing adultery and shouting at her, it is not enough that he simply acknowledges one fault, such as the shouting, without also acknowledging the adultery. In the case of a personal relationship to God, in which, of course, we cannot hide what we do from God, God wants us to acknowledge our sins as part of the process of reconciliation. In the sacrament of Confession, we therefore need to confess the kinds of sin we have committed and the number of times we have committed them, as well as we can remember. Note that a tendency to sin (a vice) is a disorder, but is not, properly speaking, a sin unless we surrender to the vice by some action or omission.

Should I go to Confession even if I expect to sin again?

We cannot receive absolution while actually intending to sin again, because this action would imply rejecting and accepting sin at the same time, which is a contradiction. Similarly, we cannot have a merely half-hearted commitment to avoid some sin in the future, because this would imply that our repentance from our previous sins was also half-hearted. We can, however, receive absolution even while recognising that we have a disposition to sin in some way (in other words, a vice) provided we have a firm intention not to sin again. Indeed, Confession is encouraged under such circumstances as it is a great help in fighting to eradicate such vices.

Isn't it unhealthy to bring to light what is past? Shouldn't I just move on?

What is in the past, especially serious sin, can continue to poison the present – like a wound that festers in a way that is invisible to the eye. It is only by bringing the damage to light that healing is possible. Furthermore, serious sin is like an infidelity in marriage. Just as an act of reconciliation with one's spouse may be necessary before it is possible to move on, so also in the case of one's relationship to God. It is not until one receives the Sacrament of Confession, also and appropriately called 'Reconciliation', that one can move on.

I have never been to Confession and I am simply nervous. What should I do?

Confession is surprisingly straightforward: all that one really needs is a readiness to state one's sins with the firm intention not to sin again. With regard to the rite itself, one can always ask the priest for help and the priest will be very willing to guide those who are unfamiliar with the sacrament or who have been away from the sacrament for a long time. Both God and the priest welcome sinners with joy and will think well of those who are humble enough and honest enough to seek reconciliation through this sacrament. Furthermore, the priest is bound by a seal of absolute secrecy. He will not be shocked by sins, and, as a sinner, goes to Confession himself.

For those who are nervous, a traditional confessional, in which priest and penitent are separated by a grill or lattice, provides anonymity that makes the practice of this sacrament easier for many people. It may also be encouraging to hear some personal testimonies and stories from the lives of the saints that testify to the power and healing of Confession.

Is Confession confidential?

Confession is absolutely confidential. The priest is forbidden to reveal any sins confessed under the seal of Confession, even when facing threats to his life or that of others – at the risk of losing his own soul. The Church even venerates a martyr to the seal of Confession, St John of Nepomuk (d. 1393), who is said to have been killed by the king of Bohemia after refusing to disclose the sins confessed by the queen.

Further reading. *Compendium* questions 296-312 (the sacrament of Confession) and 434-533 (the Commandments); *Catechism* ccc. 1422-1498 and 2052-2557, especially: (i) the acts of the penitent (ccc. 1450-1460); (ii) the effects of the sacrament (ccc. 1468-1470); (iii) the celebration of the sacrament (ccc. 1480-1484).

The Virgin in Prayer by Sassoferrato

Mary is especially venerated among all the saints. She is our heavenly mother, accepted by St John on our behalf as the final gift of Christ from the cross before his death, *"Then he said to the disciple, 'Behold, your mother!'"* (Jn 19:27)

Catholic Devotions

A devotion is a customary popular prayer, often linked to other holy actions, objects or places.

Do devotions that are directed to Mary and the saints detract from the worship of God?

Devotions to Mary and the saints do not detract from the worship of God. Devotions express love, but love is not a finite good such as a cake, where a larger slice for one person means a smaller slice for everyone else. On the contrary, love multiplies when it is shared, and to love Mary and the saints gives even more glory to God who created them and saved them. Furthermore, the saints, through their immense variety, glorify many manifestations of God's creativity and saving love, expanding our knowledge and love of God. Finally, the saints are the friends of God in the glory of heaven. Just as one does not experience a slight to oneself when one's beloved friends are also honoured, God is pleased and not angered by honour given to his saints.

As a Catholic, am I obliged to practise some devotions?

While no Catholic is obliged to practise any particular devotion, there is strong evidence that a devotional life of *some* kind is practically essential for a fruitful Christian life. Proof of this assertion can be found in the decrees of the

Second Ecumenical Council of Nicaea in 787 AD. This council mandated the use and reverence of holy images (of Jesus, Mary and the saints) *"on the walls of churches, in the homes, and in all conspicuous places, by the roadside and everywhere."* In other words, the Council stated that a normal Christian life should be characterised by various devotions, associated with conspicuous holy images in private and public spaces.

I am uncomfortable with the physical aspects of devotions, like Rosary beads, crucifixes and pictures. What would you say to reassure me about these practices?

The physical, tangible and visual aspects of devotions are important because they flow from the central truth of the Christianity – that God became a man like us, that is, body and soul. Christianity is, therefore, a *physical* faith because of Christ, and not just a matter of abstract words and thoughts. In the early Church, Tertullian articulated this principle with the following words, *"The flesh is the hinge of salvation"* (De res. 8, 2: PL 2, 852). The importance of tangible expressions of the faith is also shown by the fact that societies that reject such expressions also tend, subsequently, to decline in Christian belief. The Puritan movement in England, for example, which destroyed much medieval devotional art, did not produce an enduring form of Christian life but may, in retrospect, have paved the way for secularism. Finally, it is notable that political and religious movements hostile to Christianity have an especial dislike for tangible symbols of the faith: there are countries today, for example, where it is even forbidden to wear a small cross. The peculiar hatred of these tangible symbols is strong indirect evidence of their importance.

Could you illustrate the benefits of devotions a little more clearly?

One of the clearest illustrations of the benefits of devotions is that many of the greatest saints had a strong devotional life. St Padre Pio, for example, prayed the Rosary almost continuously. Further evidence of the importance of devotions can be seen in the lives of recent Popes. Pope John Paul II, for example, remarked that reading the *True Devotion to Mary* by St Louis-Marie de Montfort was a 'decisive turning point' in his life. Devotions have also been fruitful for art and music. The source and original motivation of so much Western art can be found in the desire to express the 'concretely given supernatural', such as devotional images of Jesus, Mary and the saints. Devotions have also influenced music. The *Hail Mary*, for example, has been set to music by Brahms, Byrd, Elgar, Mozart, Rossini, Saint-Saëns, Verdi and many others. So devotions have had a demonstrably fruitful impact on the world. Finally, besides helping us to grow in holiness and enriching our culture, devotions are a source of practical daily help. A key Scriptural text here is the miracle at Cana (Jn 2:1-11), when Jesus turned water into wine following his mother's request for help. This event teaches us that God will answer prayers offered by the saints on our behalf and, especially, the prayers of Mary, the Mother of God.

Further reading. *Compendium* questions 351-353 and 557-566; *Catechism* ccc. 2650-2696 covering especially (i) the tradition of prayer (ccc. 2650-2662); (ii) the way of prayer (ccc. 2663-2682); (iii) guides for prayer (ccc. 2683-2696).

Catechism of the Catholic Church

First Presented to the Faithful of the World
by Pope John Paul II, 11 October 1992

"A full, complete exposition of Catholic doctrine, enabling everyone to know what the Church professes, celebrates, lives and prays in her daily life."

Laetarum magnopere, 15 August 1997

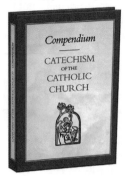

Compendium of the Catechism

Promulgated by Pope Benedict XVI
28 June 2005

"A faithful and sure synthesis of the Catechism of the Catholic Church."

Further Reading

Pope John Paul II declared the *Catechism of the Catholic Church* (1992) to be the sure and authentic reference text for all local catechisms. This compilation of further reading gives cross-references to the *Catechism* and to the *Compendium* (2005), the official synthesis of the *Catechism*.

SECTION		CATECHISM PARAGRAPHS	COMPENDIUM QUESTIONS
1	The Meaning of Life	27-49	1-5
2	Creation and Fall	279-421	51-78
3	Salvation History	50-64	6-8; 102
4	The Incarnation	422-486	79-104
5	The Life of Christ	512-570	105-111
6	The Paschal Mystery	571-667	112-132
7	The Trinity	199-267; 687-747	33-50; 136-146
8	The Church	748-962	147-195
9	Scripture and Tradition	74-141	6-24
10	Mary and the Four Last Things	964-975; 988-1060	94-100, 133-135, 196-199; 202-216

SECTION	CATECHISM PARAGRAPHS	COMPENDIUM QUESTIONS
11 Liturgy and Sacraments	1066-1211	218-250
12 Baptism and Confirmation	1213-1284; 1285-1321	251-270
13 The Eucharist	1322-1419	271-294
14 Confession and Anointing	1420-1532	295-320
15 Marriage and Holy Orders	1533-1666	321-350
16 Moral Action	407-409; 1264; 1730-1748; 1749-1761; 1776-1802; 1846-1876	363-376; 391-400
17 Natural Law and the Ten Commandments	1949-1964; 2052-2557	415-421; 434-533
18 Grace and the Beatitudes	1716-1729; 1812-1835; 1987-2029	358-362; 384-390; 422-428
19 Virtues and Vices	1803-1829; 1833-1844	377-383
20 Christian Life in the World	1877-1948; 2012-2016; 2041-2043; 2201-2246; 2270-2283; 2351-2400	401-414; 428-433
21 The Life of Prayer	2558-2758	534-556; 567-577
22 The Lord's Prayer	2759-2865	578-598
23 Praying the Mass	1345-1355	271-294
24 The Practice of Confession	1422-1498; 2052-2557	296-312; 434-533
25 Catholic Devotions	2650-2696	351-353; 557-566

Subject Index

This index lists the key pages for each topic. More detailed explanations can be found in the *Catechism of the Catholic Church* and the *Compendium*.

For further information on the topics
covered in this booklet, see also:

CREDO

The Catholic Faith Explained

*A new, illustrated, pocket catechism offering a succinct and
reliable introduction into the fullness of the Catholic faith.*

*Credo draws on Scripture and Tradition, and is fully cross
referenced to the Catechism and Compendium.*

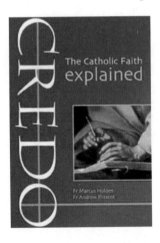

Available from the Catholic Truth Society